ANCIENT CHINA'S
MYTHS AND BELIEFS

ANCIENT CHINA'S
MYTHS AND BELIEFS

Tony Allan and Charles Phillips

ROSEN
PUBLISHING®

New York

This edition published in 2012 by:

The Rosen Publishing Group, Inc.
29 East 21st Street
New York, NY 10010

Library of Congress Cataloging-in Publication Data

Allan, Tony, 1946–
Ancient China's myths and beliefs/Tony Allan, Charles Phillips.
    p. cm.—(World mythologies)
Includes bibliographical references (p.   ) and index.
✓ISBN 978-1-4488-5991-7 (library binding)
1. Mythology, Chinese. 2. China—Religion. I. Phillips, Charles. II. Title.
BL1825.A45 2012
299.5'1113—dc23

                                                                    2011036528

Manufactured in the United States of America

CPSIA Compliance Information: Batch #W12YA. For further information, contact Rosen Publishing, New York, New York, at 1-800-237-9932.

Series copyright © 1999 Time-Life Books
Text copyright © 1999 Duncan Baird Publishers
Design and artwork copyright © 1999 Duncan Baird Publishers

Metric Conversion Chart

1 inch = 2.54 centimeters
1 foot = 30.48 centimeters
1 yard = .914 meters
1 square foot = .093 square meters
1 square mile = 2.59 square kilometers
1 ton = .907 metric tons
1 pound = 454 grams
1 mile = 1.609 kilometers

Contents

A rare 14th-century red lacquer dish by Zhou Ming, decorated with Buddhistic lions.

ANCIENT DYNASTIES

Clad in robes of green and yellow, the colors of the ripening crop, the emperor cut a splendid figure as he raised his arms up to the skies. Who but he, the Son of Heaven, could address his celestial forefathers on behalf of the Chinese nation? And if through some calamity he failed to repeat the time-honored formulas, would the heavens not avenge the slight by sending disaster on his people? So, for more than three millennia, rulers of the most populous nation on Earth offered prayers and sacrifices to the gods and plowed the first furrow of each new agricultural year.

Politically the emperor dominated China, and in its religion he served as a living link with the heavens. In a tightly governed nation, the gods themselves sometimes seemed like divine bureaucrats whose powers mimicked imperial rule on Earth. Some texts even spoke of a heavenly Ministry of Thunder, with a staff of emissaries waiting, for all the world like the emperor's own officials, to carry out the edicts of the bird-headed Thunder God.

Yet this ordered cosmology was only part of a many-faceted world of myth almost as multifarious as the Chinese people themselves were numerous. In the confusion of conflicting beliefs, some strands stand out. Among the earliest ingredients was ancestor worship, posited on the belief that a part of the human soul survived death; if sustained by sacrifices, it would repay kinfolk by bringing good fortune to the family and providing advice through divination. Another was the brand of ritual practiced in early times by wu shamans. Much of their magic was subsequently taken up by Daoist priests, who added concerns with the right diet and breathing in their quest for the way to achieve harmony with the physical universe. In later times, too, Buddhism would bring its own distinctive philosophy.

The most substantial corpus of myth, however, was pseudo-historical and related to the period before the beginnings of recorded time. Perhaps it is not surprising that a nation with a longer dynastic record than any other should have chosen to extend the account backward into myth. So the pageant of Chinese legend merges with the actual past, and mythical kings such as the Yellow Emperor and serpent-bodied Fu Xi take their place in a line of rulers that ran all the way up to the last emperor, forced to abdicate in 1912.

Above: A 19th-century greenish-gold Dragon Robe of embroidered silk. The splendor of this robe suggests an owner of high status, near the apex of Chinese society.

Opposite: The Great Wall was first built in 214 BCE, just seven years after China's unification. At more than 4,000 kilometers, the wall is the longest stone structure ever made and links a series of older walls built to protect against marauding nomads.

7

The First Chinese

The human presence goes back a long way in China. In 1927, scientists investigating a site at Zhoukoudian, not far from the city now known as Beijing, found the first remains of so-called Peking Man. Other finds followed before the excavation was closed by warfare in 1938, by which time it was realized that these were the vestiges of a community of hunter-gatherers dating back 460,000 years. They belonged to the species *Homo erectus*.

Unlike *Ramapithecus*, a predecessor of the great apes found in China and much of the Eurasian landmass as much as 10 million years before, *Homo erectus* walked on two legs, as its name implies. These hominids proved remarkably adaptable in the face of the fierce climate changes of the epoch in which they lived. If subsequent discoveries suggesting that they first appeared in China as much as 1.7 million years ago are correct, they must have survived the chill of two Ice Ages as well as the warm and moist conditions of the intervening inter-glacial period.

The earliest settlements in China were along the middle reaches of the Yellow River where the rich, fertile loess enabled agriculture to take place using simple tools.

There is a huge chronological gap separating Zhoukoudian from the next early communities to have been studied in detail. These date from around 5000 BCE, and reveal that, after a million years of nomadic hunting and gathering, *Homo sapiens* had taken the giant leap into life in settled communities supported by the cultivation of crops. These distant ancestors built dwellings along the fertile banks of the Yellow River in central China and south in the great delta of the Yangtzi. They grew millet and soybeans, and by around 4000 BCE they had domesticated wild rice.

The earliest rice cultivators in the Yangtzi Delta created artificial pools or paddies in which to grow their crops. Rice-growing was labor-intensive, requiring the joint efforts of many individuals to transplant the seedlings from dry land to the growing areas and then to pick the grain. As cultivation spread across the rest of the country, a tradition of communal endeavor went with it. Villages with as many as 600 inhabitants were built during this period of so-called Yangshao culture, the name deriving from a village in Henan Province where evidence of settled life first surfaced in 1921. The dwellings were single-room huts made of mud and straw, their floors often sunk well below ground level, with central hearths and thatched roofs.

By swelling food supplies, the coming of agriculture encouraged population growth. Even so, harvests were uncertain enough to drive farmers to oracles to find out what the future would bring. The form of prediction they favored was scapulimancy, which involved heating tortoise shells or animal bones – shoulder-blades were preferred – and studying the resulting cracks for information about what would happen next. Early on, diviners started carving marks on the bones to assist their prognostications. These symbols played a major part in the development of Chinese writing.

The Longshan period followed the Yangshao. Villagers began to build fortifications and learned to use the potter's wheel. One village dating from the period was rimmed with ramparts of compacted earth as much as eight meters wide at their base. Within these defensive fortifications many stone arrowheads and spear-tips have been found. The arts of peace also progressed. A distinctive feature of this culture is its delicate pottery. This era also provides the first direct evidence of another long-standing Chinese tradition: ancestor worship. At the time the dead were buried within settlement walls and often under the floors of houses. In the patrilinear society of the day, the emphasis of the cult was strongly male. From about 3000 BCE ceramic phallic symbols were made,

This map of China shows provincial boundaries under the Ming dynasty in about 1550. The Great Wall, extended during the Qin dynasty, protects the northern frontier and the Grand Canal, built during the later Sui dynasty, links the Yellow and Yangtzi rivers in the north and south respectively.

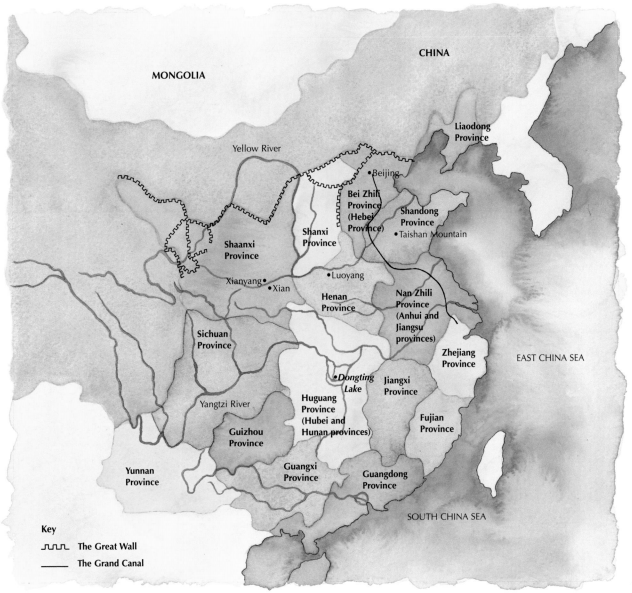

Key

ᒐᒐ The Great Wall

—— The Grand Canal

9

Bloody Rites for the Royal Dead

Archaeological excavations have shown that human sacrifice was once practiced in China, and that in the Shang period the nation's rulers did not go to Heaven alone.

The tombs of eleven of the twelve Shang kings lie near the royal capital of Anyang, in the Yellow River valley south of Beijing. The rulers were interred in lacquered wooden chambers at the bottom of grave pits up to twelve meters deep. Four long earthen ramps, dug in the shape of a cross, led down to the tomb. In one of the pits, the remains of nine armed men were found below the floor of the tomb chamber itself. Alongside them were dog bones, suggesting that soldiers and watchdogs were sacrificed before the ceremony to serve as sentinels for the monarch after death. After the corpse had been laid to rest, rich grave goods were deposited in the tomb and further human sacrifices made.

A tiger protects a man, a guardian for the afterlife. This Shang-period vessel is decorated with magical motifs.

seemingly with ritual or magical significance. When writing began in the second millennium BCE, the Chinese character used to indicate an ancestor was a representation of the male member.

Recently Chinese archaeologists have been eagerly scanning late Longshan sites for signs of the legendary Xia dynasty, which early Chinese chroniclers claimed to have been the first in their country's history. So far no definite evidence has been found to prove it ever really existed, leaving only literary sources dating from more than a millennium later to argue its case. But with the Shang dynasty, which succeeded the Xia, events move out of the world of legend and into history. The date of 1766 BCE, traditionally given for its start, roughly coincides with the first appearance of bronze in China, and the Shang rulers were Bronze-Age monarchs in the manner of the Homeric kings of Mycenaean Greece. Like Homer's heroes, they swept across battlefields on chariots and used expensive metal weapons to enforce their rule. They reigned from fortress-palaces, and their deaths were marked by grandiose funeral rites.

Social divisions that were becoming apparent in the preceding Longshan era widened under the Shang. Already at Chengziyai the graves of dead villagers suggest marked differences in wealth. While most people were buried without coffins in narrow pits with at best a few simple grave goods, a privileged minority were interred in caskets inside large tombs adorned with elegant jade ornaments and finely crafted ceramics. Inequality increased as villages gave way to towns, providing new opportunities for craftsmen, traders and administrators. By Shang times the social hierarchy extended from a warrior aristocracy with close family connections to the monarchy down to a slave class. Most of the bondsmen were non-Chinese captives taken in warfare beyond the Shang's northern and western borders. Marked out from others by a special hair braid, they worked as nobles' servants, grooms and gardeners. Captives sometimes suffered a worse fate, for archaeological finds indicate that the era saw an upsurge in human sacrifice.

The Shang rulers also made more positive contributions to Chinese society that won them a reputation in later times as enlightened sage-kings. It was in their day that writing developed (see box, page 13) and an accurate calendar was prepared. Above all, they created a centralized realm. From their heartland in the North China plain, the monarchs spread their rule over perhaps as much as

A late Shang-period (13th–12th century BCE) container for fragrant wine offered to ancestors, from the tomb of a king of the bird clan.

100,000 square kilometers of northern China, embracing all the lands north of the Yangtzi River.

The lynchpin of the Shang system was the emperor, whose significance in the cosmic scheme of things was more than merely mortal. He also took on a religious role as an intermediary between his people and the gods. Tracing his own descent from Shangdi, the ruler of the natural world, he performed essential rituals to appease his divine ancestor and to persuade the other gods of the Chinese pantheon to look down with favor on his people. From this early time the nation's rulers acquired a more-than-human aura as semi-divine beings entrusted with the Mandate of Heaven.

According to tradition, the Shang era came to an end in 1027 BCE, when its hated last monarch, Zhou Xin, lost his throne to the more virtuous Wu, the founder of the Zhou dynasty. The histories moralized his fall, claiming he was infatuated by his beautiful wife Dan Ji, who, it was said, delighted in inventing sadistic tortures that were inflicted on those who fell foul of her. As a consequence, few mourned the overthrow of the royal couple.

The new dynasty was, in name at least, the longest-lasting in Chinese history, and its early rulers presided over the full flowering of the nation's feudal order. As the Bronze Age gave way to the Iron Age, the warrior nobility lost their monopoly of metal weapons and the nature of warfare gradually changed from an aristocratic pursuit to a clash of massed armies. The slave class that had existed in the Shang world also largely disappeared. Instead, society became stratified into an economic pyramid, with the king and nobles at the top and a base provided by the nation's millions of peasant farmers. This agricultural labor force not only produced the surpluses

11

Later artists were fascinated by the legendary kings of the Zhou dynasty, whose time was regarded as a golden era. This 17th- or 18th-century woodblock print is of King Wen, one of the dynasty's founders.

of food China needed to exist, but also provided a vast pool of unpaid labor for public works and, at times of year when there was relatively little to do on the land, it constituted the backbone of the royal army.

The ideological underpinning of the system lay in the idea that all landed property was ultimately royal. The ruler held the kingdom in trust from the gods as an essential prop of celestial and Earthly order, and in return he was expected to watch over his subjects' well-being. Like the feudal system that flourished in Europe 2,000 years later, the Chinese system was open to abuse. At its best, however, it provided security and stability in uncertain times. In later years, order-loving philosophers would look back to the early Zhou era in a glow of nostalgia. They preferred to picture it as a golden age when benevolent noblemen watched over the well-being of those who worked the lands around their manors; a period when master and serf were bound by ties of mutual respect and obligation.

Chinese religion was also taking shape at this time. Human sacrifice gradually fell out of favor but the cult of the royal ancestors survived undiminished and much care was taken over preparing food for them in magnificent bronze vessels. Zhou emperors also worshipped the earth, taking pains to propitiate agrarian deities such as Houtu, the soil god, and Houji, the deity responsible for grain. Divination continued to be important, and its techniques were extended to include the drawing of lots. The oracular *Yi Jing* (*I Ching* or *Book of Changes*) – according to tradition, written by the father of the first Zhou king, Wu – also dates from this time, and rulers sought its advice by constructing hexagrams selected by throwing yarrow stalks. Ordinary people turned to sorcerers to placate the malignant spirits they blamed for their misfortunes and also to consult the spirits of ancestors for advice and prognostication.

For all its initial strength, the Zhou dynasty eventually fell victim to the problems inherent in every feudal monarchy. In its first, expansionist years, its rulers bound freshly conquered lands to them by appointing kinsmen to rule their new subjects. In time, however, the bonds of family loyalty weakened and the provinces broke away. And like all autocrats, the kings were vulnerable to trouble closer to home in the form of court intrigue.

Things came to a head in 771 BCE, when the ruling monarch, You, put aside his legitimate heir in favor of the son of a concubine. Siding with the aggrieved wife, disgruntled noblemen allied themselves with nomadic tribesmen from beyond the imperial borders to overthrow him. The ruler was slain and his capital was sacked. The victors then set up the disinherited son in a new capital, Luoyang, 350 kilometers to the east.

The new Zhou king owed his throne to the rebel lords, and they never let him forget that fact. In effect, the debacle marked the end of the Zhou dynasty as China's ruling power. Though the so-called Eastern Zhou kings continued nominally to rule the country for a further 550 years, their political influence steadily eroded until they controlled nothing but a small, impoverished territory around their capital. What prestige they retained was largely religious, for they continued to perform rituals and conduct ceremonies in the name of all the Chinese people.

Chinese Writing

The Chinese invented writing independently, without any knowledge of developments elsewhere in the world, and the art of writing – or calligraphy – is highly regarded; alongside painting it is seen as the purest of arts.

Chinese writing seems to have developed early in the second millennium BCE, probably from the symbols carved by diviners on oracle bones. Initially the 3,500 or so characters were used in the form of inscriptions, either on the bones themselves or on bronze vessels. With the introduction of the writing brush around the turn of the first millennium BCE, however, works started to be written on strips of bamboo. Rolls of silk were used from the second century BCE onward, and paper was in existence in 105 CE.

At first Chinese characters were pictographic, but a phonetic element soon crept in to accommodate concepts that could not easily be shown pictorially. Many similar-sounding words ended up resembling one another, however, so in the year 213 BCE the characters were adjusted by adding new strokes to reduce the risk of ambiguity. This reformed script has remained the basis of written Chinese to the present day, and until recent times it was the world's most widely published language.

Nobles at War

In the Spring and Autumn period – so called from the chronicle of that name covering events in the state of Lu from 722 BCE to 481 BCE – real power passed to a succession of great noblemen who maintained a balance of power among the rival fiefdoms by force of arms. This was a demanding occupation: the best-known such overlord, Duke Huan of Qi, went to war no less than twenty-eight times in forty-two years.

Warfare remained a largely aristocratic pursuit to judge from a famous anecdote of the time. This describes how three noble warriors from the state of Chu taunted their foe on the battlefield by speeding past their ranks in a chariot, loosing off arrows. When a group of enemy charioteers took up the pursuit, the trio headed back toward their own lines, only to pause when a stag broke cover in order to bring the beast down. Halting to retrieve their quarry, they presented it as a gift to their pursuers, who duly called off the chase.

Even so, war played a serious role in concentrating power in the hands of the great lords. According to the *Book of Rites*, there were 1,763 separate imperial fiefdoms in the Western Zhou period but fewer than twenty remained by 500 BCE. Those that survived were tightly organized military powers, constantly on the watch for the threat of invasion by their neighbors. The stage was set for the next era of Chinese history, the age of Warring States.

This epoch, which ended when imperial unification was finally achieved in 221 BCE, left a lasting impression on the Chinese psyche. The times were all too obviously out of joint. From the twenty statelets that survived in the year 500 BCE, seven emerged as serious contenders for supremacy. For almost three centuries they jockeyed for

A plateau area in the Xinjiang region where warfare between tribal groups often disrupted the normal pattern of life. Such lawlessness was visited upon most of China during the feudal wars of the Spring and Autumn period.

14

position, forming alliances of convenience and then treacherously breaking them, disrupting the settled patterns of agricultural life with fire and the sword.

This was a time of deep insecurity when technological and economic change were revolutionizing the nature of Chinese society. The feudal system was eroded by the demands of war. As land ownership became concentrated in fewer and fewer hands, the old link between master and peasant was weakened. The problems of debt and violent death joined the ever-present threat of bad harvests and famine in the peasant's litany of woe.

A bronze helmet dating from the Zhou dynasty, the decline of which led to the Warring States period (481 BCE–221 BCE) when China was torn apart by battles fought between warlords.

The New Rich
At the same time, trade was thriving, stimulated by a growing population and the diminishing self-sufficiency of the feudal estates. The new class of merchants was despised by the old landed aristocracy, who passed laws preventing traders from taking up official posts. Such measures failed to stop them getting wealthy, however, and they found a base for themselves in the towns that were sprouting on the major trading routes, often growing up around the fortresses of local rulers. Another innovation that benefited commerce was the introduction of metal coins, which around this time began to replace such unsatisfactory currencies as cowrie shells and bales of silk as a medium of exchange.

Unexpectedly, this dynamic, dangerous world saw an upsurge in learning and literary activity. The so-called "Hundred Schools" of philosophy came into being as wandering teachers, mostly drawn from the *shi* class of lesser landowners and administrators, each came up with their own

intellectual solutions to the manifold problems of the age. In the long term, just two voices were to dominate the babel of conflicting theories, though neither won very much recognition at the time. One of these voices was that of Kongfuzi, or "Master Kong," better known in the West by the Latinized name of Confucius.

Confucius
Born in 551 BCE in the small northeastern state of Lu, Confucius came from a noble family that had seen better days, though his father was reputedly a brave warrior. Already seventy when his son was conceived, the old man died soon after his birth, leaving Confucius to be brought up by his mother. In his teens, the future philosopher took administrative jobs, managing stables and keeping books for a state-owned granary. He is also said to have married at this time and to have fathered a son, but little else is known of his family life. His mother died when he was in his mid-twenties, and he mourned her loss for three years as custom demanded, leaving the bottom of his robe unhemmed as a token of grief. Soon afterward he gave up his job to devote his career to teaching. At the time there was a constant demand for men of learning to tutor administrators for the rival states.

What Confucius had to offer his charges was a profoundly conservative vision of society. Like other thinkers born in troubled times, he saw the solution to the world's problems in a return to order, which meant an acceptance of social hierarchies: "Let the ruler be a ruler and the subject a subject; let the father be a father and the son a son." The corollary of such compliance was that

15

those in power must show generosity of spirit to their underlings. To carry out their duties properly, they must practice self-discipline and study widely to achieve a suitable breadth of vision. His advice to a ruler was: "Approach your duties with reverence and be trustworthy in what you say; avoid excesses in expenditure and love your fellow men; employ the labor of the common people only in the proper seasons."

In domestic life, Confucius stressed the importance of following the traditional rituals by which children showed respect for their parents and parents for the ancestors who had gone before. As for the religious beliefs on which ceremonies were based, Confucius remained vague, telling a disciple who asked him about the after-life, "You do not understand even life, so how can you understand death?" His concern was always with the social rather than the supernatural world.

Even so, he played an important role in the story of Chinese myth because it was for the most part his disciples who collected and recorded the stories of long-ago kings that form much of the country's classical heritage. Confucius himself often cited these legendary monarchs as examples of good or bad governance.

Although he had attracted only a small band of devoted followers by the time of his death in 479 BCE (one source numbered them at 3,000), his long-term influence was powerful, for in time his doctrine of respect for order would win official approval as the closest thing to a state ideology that China was to know.

Confucius's name is indelibly linked with the so-called "Five Classics," ancient texts that were revered by Confucians as the font of wisdom and the foundation of scholarship. Of these, the *Shu Jing* or *Book of History* is a collection of documents that forms the chief source of information on the earliest period of Chinese history, including the legendary Xia dynasty. The *Yi Jing* or *Book of Changes* contains cryptic oracular pronouncements, while the *Shi Jing* (*Book of Poetry*) is the first anthology of Chinese poems, some of which are thought to have been written as early as 1000 BCE. The other two works are the *Li Ji* or *Book of Rites*, and the *Chun Qiu* – literally *Spring and Autumn* – which tells the history of Confucius's native state of Lu from 722 BCE to 481 BCE in chronicle form.

All five works were associated with Confucius, who may have written the *Spring and Autumn* and was long thought to have edited the others. After the sage's death they became the basic texts of the educational system developed in his name. When, in the second century BCE, Han

An early 18th-century interpretation of a scene from the life of Confucius and his disciples. Confucius was opposed to the putting of straw models of people in tombs for fear that it would lead to human sacrifice.

emperors made Confucianism the official doctrine of their empire, the Five Classics formed the core curriculum of academic study. As a result, the works' influence was immense.

The Way and its Power

The Confucian civic-minded doctrine of altruistic morality and social responsibility was ideally suited to a populous and carefully governed nation, but it had little to offer those seeking individual salvation. As if to complement it, a second philosophical movement began at much the same time that appealed to exactly the people that the sage's aphorisms failed to satisfy. This was Daoism, and its prophet was Laozi.

Almost nothing is known of Laozi's life, though one tradition maintains that he was born in 604 BCE and earned his living as a librarian in the Zhou imperial household. The work for which he is remembered, the *Dao De Jing* or the *Way and its Power*, is less a philosophical treatise than a collection of aphorisms or short poems written by someone with a taste for paradox; in fact many scholars now consider it the work of more than one hand. Yet two sentiments that ring out loudly from it are a preference for nature and solitude over human society and an emphasis on *rang* or yieldingness, the quality suggested by the modern phrase "Go with the flow." "The wise man," Laozi wrote, "keeps to the deed that consists in taking no action." If the poetic force of the *Dao De Jing*

ensured an audience for its sayings, their cryptic nature allowed Laozi's followers to interpret them much as they wished. In fact the Daoist religion, which evolved gradually over the next millennium, embraced mysticism, magic and a return to nature. In its rejection of the worldly it helped to prepare the way for Buddhism.

While the philosophers of the Hundred Schools argued, the rulers of the Warring States schemed and fought. Foot soldiers had by now replaced war chariots as the decisive battlefield force, and as the stakes rose higher ever larger armies were needed to stay in the game. By the fourth century BCE, each of the leading powers, Qin and Chu, could put more than a million men in the field. Death tolls rose accordingly: at Chang Ping in 260 BCE Qin commanders reportedly ordered the slaughter of more than 400,000 prisoners of war.

Partly as a result of its single-minded ruthlessness, Qin – the easternmost of the states, regarded as little better than barbarian by the others – eventually emerged triumphant from the bloodletting. When its armies overran the last of its rivals in 221 BCE, China was finally reunited.

The First Emperor

The ruler who achieved victory took the name of Shi Huangdi, the First Emperor, and he was to prove one of history's most terrifyingly effective autocrats. As ruler of Qin he had been fortunate to survive an assassination attempt made with a poisoned dagger, and ever afterward he was distrustful of those around him.

The First Emperor has never been much loved in China. Intellectuals have good reason to remember him with hatred, for it was in his reign that the infamous Burning of the Books took place. Fearing the subversive impact of the nation's disputatious philosophers, the emperor gave orders that all works except historical records and treatises on medicine, agriculture and divination should be destroyed. Individual scholars fared even worse:

Laozi believed that people should live harmoniously alongside animals, perhaps the reason he is often shown mounted on a buffalo, as in this bronze statuette. His belief in not disrupting the balance of the natural world was a reaction to the troubled times in which he lived.

The Five Elements

Following an ancient religious tradition, the Chinese believed that the world was composed of five basic elements, not the four of Western convention. The quintet had mystical significance, and the workings of the universe were explained by their interaction.

The five elements were earth, wood, metal, fire and water, and they were thought to succeed one another in an unending cycle of creation and destruction. Philosophers maintained that the vital matter that was the essence of all being was transformed through the working of yang and yin – the complementary forces of action and passivity – into the elements, which in their turn became the building blocks of the physical universe.

The concept, which was mentioned in the earliest texts, was elaborated in the course of the first millennium BCE as an explanation of the cycle of change in the Earth and the heavens, and so as one of the fundamental factors affecting people's fate. Sages who could understand the cycle of the elements were thought to have the power to foresee future events. Even the rise and fall of dynasties could be linked to their interplay.

The Chinese zodiac, shown on this bronze disk, was given an extra dimension by the Five Elements theory. Each year was associated with an element as well as one of 12 animals; so for example, a person born in a horse year – which came around every 12 years – was potentially a fire horse only once every 60 years.

460 of them were executed by imperial command. Another charge brought against the monarch was that he was obsessed by superstition. In thrall to the Five Elements theory (see box above), he became convinced that water, the sign of the Qin dynasty, could predominate only if a policy of brutal repression was pursued. He was also fascinated by the notion of an elixir of life, and in 219 BCE, on the advice of his diviners, he sent 3,000 young people to find the magic potion on an imagined "Island of Immortals" thought to lie across the Eastern Sea. None was ever seen again, though later legends claimed that they settled in Japan.

Yet for all his failings, the First Emperor's achievements were on an astonishing scale. It was he who built the Great Wall by linking existing defenses into a continuous fortification snaking for more than 5,000 kilometers along the nation's northern and eastern frontiers. Amazingly the work, involving many millions of man-hours, was completed in just seven years. Other major civil-engineering projects included the Magic Transport Canal, a thirty-two-kilometer channel across central China that opened up 2,000 kilometers of waterway, parts of which are still in use today.

Shi Huangdi's work in unifying the country was to prove almost as enduring. To bind the conquered lands together he reformed the written language, creating a core vocabulary of about 3,000 universally accepted characters. He imposed a uniformly harsh legal code on all his dominions, and standardized weights, measures and even the width of wagon axles, so that carts all over China could trundle along equidistantly spaced ruts. He also set about dismantling China's feudal power structure by forcing all the noble families of the provinces to move to his capital at Xianyang, where he could keep a close eye on them.

His final endeavor, on a scale with anything he had done earlier in his career, was the construction of his own tomb, which remains for the most part unexcavated to this day. Expecting to be emperor of China in the afterlife also, he had a model of his kingdom constructed underground,

The infamous book burning that took place during the reign of the First Emperor, Shi Huangdi, was commemorated by later artists. This painting, dating from the Qing dynasty (1644–1912), also shows scholars being buried alive. Although he suppressed the many schools of thought, the First Emperor also imposed a system of writing and weights and measures that accelerated both the process and sense of national unification.

complete with mercury-filled channels mimicking the Yangtzi and Yellow rivers and a starry firmament set with pearls. Booby-trapped crossbows guarded the sepulchre from human intruders, while protection for the emperor in the afterlife was provided by thousands of lifesize model soldiers buried in four pits a kilometer to the east of the tomb. This was the famous Terracotta Army discovered in 1974 and made up of more than 6,000 human figures drawn up in military formation. Though molds were used to make the bodies, the faces of the guards were all sculpted individually. Sentinels for eternity, they were equipped with real weapons made from a special alloy that remains sharp and shiny to this day.

When Shi Huangdi was laid to rest in 210 BCE, a fundamental weakness in his system became apparent. Like most autocracies, it had no satisfactory mechanism for the peaceful transfer of power. The ruling family quickly split apart in a confusion of puppet emperors, overreaching ministers and squabbling court eunuchs. Eventually, the people rose up in a series of rebellions that culminated in the seizure of power by the guerrilla leader Liu Bang, founder of the Han dynasty.

The Han Era

The Han era, from 206 BCE to CE 220, is remembered in China as a time of power and glory. Among its achievements were the extension of China's borders to their present limits and even beyond into what are now Korea and Vietnam, and the establishment of competitive examinations for candidates for civil service careers. It was also at this time that Confucianism became an official cult.

The apogee of Han rule came in the fifty-three-year reign of Wu Di, literally the "Martial Emperor." Much of his time was spent battling the Xiongnu, a fierce, horse-riding people living beyond the Great Wall who may have been ancestors of the Huns who invaded the Roman Empire five centuries later.

It was initially the quest for allies against the ferocious Xiongnu foe that led the emperor to take China's first exploratory steps toward the outside world. Wu Di's probe took the form of an embassy sent westward through Xiongnu territory. The expedition's leader, Zhang Qian, was captured and spent ten years as a prisoner before escaping to continue his mission. He finally returned to the court, Rip-van-Winkle-like, twelve years after his departure. With him he brought animal and plant specimens that included walnuts and grapevines, along with stories of a kingdom called Fergana where Chinese merchants could trade silk for horses bigger than the ponies ridden by the Xiongnu. He had in fact reached Bactria, one of the states set up in the wake of the Greek emperor Alexander the Great's epic eastward expedition, in lands that now form part of Afghanistan and Uzbekistan.

Zhang Qian's report had great significance for China, for it led ultimately to the establishment of the Silk Road and the first contacts between China and Greco-Roman civilization. Direct communication was blocked by the powerful state of Parthia, which served as a buffer, but even so the

A kneeling archer from the Terracotta Army, a 6,000-strong force of life-sized statues of soldiers, plus horses, which was buried close to the First Emperor's tomb near the city of Xian. His bow has been stolen by a grave robber.

Chinese became dimly aware of a great Western power they called Da Qin – actually the Roman Empire. At the same time the emperors established contact, via Burma, with the rulers of India and with Japan, at the time still a land of tribal villages. The Chinese world was expanding.

The last century of Han rule was a time of steadily weakening imperial authority. The throne passed to a succession of underage monarchs, and real power was vested in the hands of dowager empresses and court eunuchs, household officials whose great influence stemmed from their proximity to the monarch. While the court intrigued, provincial lords seized the opportunity to increase their authority, burdening the peasantry with additional taxes. Gradually central control collapsed, and warlords vied to extend their grip over the nation's constituent parts. In 220 CE, when the last Han emperor abdicated in favor of the son of a warlord, the empire split up into three rival kingdoms. The age of warring states had returned.

By the time of the Han dynasty's downfall, two millennia of Chinese dynastic history had already passed, and a template for the nation's

Seven Sages of the Bamboo Grove, a painting by Fu Baoshi, dating from the early part of the 20th century. The seven sages were a group of Daoist scholars who developed the Zhuangzi philosophy of *wu-wei* or "action without contrivance." Ideas continued to evolve in the Han era as China began to absorb influences from the outside world.

TIME LINE
Chinese History

Neolithic and Bronze-Age civilizations first arose in China some 7,000 years ago and were centered in the fertile areas of the middle and lower Yellow River. The two most important Neolithic cultures were the Yangshao to the west and the Longshan in the east. Bronze production on a large scale commenced during the Shang dynasty, which marked the beginning of a succession of dynastic kingships. The Qin dynasty unified the country, and the Han dynasty built upon its foundations. The Tang and, later, Ming dynasties marked golden ages for arts, crafts, manufacturing and trade. Finally, after nearly 300 years of Qing rule, the system was overthrown by republicans.

NEOLITHIC PERIOD

c. 7000 BCE *Homo sapiens* began to form settled communities and cultivate crops.
c. 5000 BCE–*c.* 3000 BCE The Yangshao culture flourished in the Yellow River region of central north China.
c. 3500 BCE–*c.* 2000 BCE The Hongshan culture flourished in northeastern China and jade carving began.
c. 3500 BCE–*c.* 2000 BCE The Liangzhu culture thrived in southeastern China.
c. 3000 BCE–*c.* 1700 BCE The Longshan culture prospered in eastern China and bronze production began at Erlitou.
c. 2000 BCE–*c.* 1800 BCE The Xia dynasty was supposedly founded by Yu the Great.

Ceremonial disks made in jade and other hard stone and dating from the Liangzhu period, *c.* 2500 BCE.

SHANG AND ZHOU DYNASTIES

c. 1800 BCE The Shang or Yin dynasty founded by Cheng Tang is the first historically authenticated dynasty. Noted for high-quality bronze work.
c. 1300 BCE Earliest surviving inscriptions on oracle bones, their sophistication indicating writing had existed for perhaps a millennium.
c. 1100 BCE Shang dynasty overthrown by Prince Wu of Zhou who established the ceremonial system later praised by Confucius. Early Zhou is now called Western Zhou.
c. 771 BCE King You of Zhou overthrown by internal revolt. Capital moved east to Luoyang, marking the beginning of Eastern Zhou.
c. 722 BCE–481 BCE Spring and Autumn period; real power passed to states established by noblemen.
c. 551 BCE Confucius born. His was the first of the Hundred Schools of thought that thrived in the Warring States period.
481 BCE–221 BCE Warring States period. Inter-state rivalry intensifies. Daoist thought develops.

future had been established. Over the remaining 1,700 years of imperial rule, periods of strong central government and outstanding cultural achievement would alternate with times of weakness when political entropy took its course and the empire disintegrated in the hands of rival warlords and tribesmen from beyond the frontiers.

The four centuries following the eclipse of the Han were something of a dark age for China, during which nomadic invaders descended upon the country from the north and the nation was for the most part politically fragmented. This time of troubles had a lasting influence on the nation's spiritual life, for the insecurity encouraged a drift from Confucianism to mystical forms of Daoism, which became firmly entrenched in the nation's consciousness. Its influence was to make itself felt in fields as diverse as painting, where it stimulated the "mountain and water" landscape style, and diet, encouraging a vogue for simple foodstuffs.

It was also at this time that Daoism acquired a rival in the form of Buddhism, imported along the Silk Road from India and central Asia. Its contemplative tranquillity offered a spiritual refuge in diffi-

cult times, while the multitude of divinities that had accumulated around it provided an alternative to the Daoist gods. The faith spread quickly in the fourth century CE; by the year 420 CE there were reportedly 1,768 monasteries in southern China alone. The loss of manpower to the cloister would eventually prove such a drain on the nation's resources that later rulers made attempts, unsuccessfully, to suppress the faith.

Unlike the Roman Empire in a similar time of trial, China eventually proved able to reunite itself, assimilating its neighboring enemies – Xiongnu, Turks, Mongols – into the mainstream of its culture. From the time of reunification in 589 CE, the nation was to know long periods of peace and progress under the Tang and Song dynasties, interrupted by bloody interludes of civil war when court intrigue ran out of hand. In this period the doctrine of Neo-Confucianism appeared, blending Confucius's moral precepts with a cosmology that drew on Daoist and Buddhist beliefs to provide a synthesis of the main currents of Chinese thought.

This happy and mostly prosperous state of affairs came to an end in 1211, when Genghis

---

EARLY DYNASTIC PERIOD

221 BCE The state of Qin under the First Emperor completed the conquest of China. He introduced harsh laws, unified weights and measures and the writing system. Work started on extending the Great Wall and digging major canals.
213 BCE All schools of thought but the Legalists were suppressed and their books banned and burned.
207 BCE Qin dynasty overthrown.
206 BCE Liu Bang founded the Han dynasty; Qin's bureaucratic system continued. Early Han known as Western.
186 BCE–140 BCE The Silk Road was opened up to the West. Confucianism favored as a state cult.
25–220 CE Han dynasty moved its capital east and the period is subsequently Eastern Han. Buddhism introduced from India.

PERIOD OF DISUNITY

228–280 Following the collapse of Han, China was divided between three warlords who founded the Wei, Shu Han and Wu kingdoms and vied with each other for overall control. The Daoist religion was founded.
317–581 The Southern and Northern dynasties. Invasions from the north and west create a series of six northern dynasties ruled by non-Chinese nomads or semi-nomads. South China remained under Chinese rule. Buddhism and Daoism grew in influence.

A fine Tang-dynasty pottery figure of a lady in profile.

MIDDLE AND LATE DYNASTIC PERIOD

A rare lime-green flask from the middle Ming period. The red dragon moon symbolizes fire.

589–618 The Sui, last of the Northern dynasties, was usurped by a general who re-established Chinese rule.
618–907 The Tang dynasty. Golden age of arts activity.
960–1279 The Song dynasty. Confucianism absorbed elements of Buddhism and Daoism.
1280–1368 The Yuan (Mongol) dynasty established. Golden age of Chinese drama.
1368–1644 The Ming dynasty restored Chinese rule with the capital in Beijing.
1644–1912 The Qing (Manchu) dynasty ruled China. Overthrown in 1912.

Khan led Mongol invaders in from the north. By 1279 his grandson Kublai Khan was in charge of the entire country. Yet again China avoided the fate of imperial Rome, managing once more to absorb its conquerors into the fabric of its own civilization. Like their Song predecessors, the emperors of the Mongol Yuan dynasty ruled luxuriously as Sons of Heaven from the city they called Dadu, today's Beijing.

Yet the Yuan rulers' discriminatory policies, favoring Mongols and other alien peoples over ethnic Chinese, roused the anger of the natives. Within a century Kublai's heirs had been driven from power by the peasant-born rebel leader Zhu Yuanzhang, founder of the Ming, or "Brilliant," dynasty. An important role in the uprising against the Yuan was played by the Pure Land sect of Buddhists, who taught that a savior known as the Maitreya, the future Buddha, would descend from Heaven to establish an Earthly paradise.

The Ming restored all the traditions of the early dynasties, including sacrifices to the gods of Earth and Heaven. Taking refuge in the past, they increasingly cut China off from the rest of the world – a policy that ultimately led to stagnation. Vigorous rule was temporarily restored in the seventeenth century under the Qing dynasty, established by Manchu conquerors from a northern homeland beyond the Great Wall. But by the late eighteenth century the nation was once more hopelessly in decline.

China, for so long the world's most advanced civilization, had become inward-looking and backward. Increasingly the past weighed as a burden on the country, stifling innovation and discouraging enterprise. Its rulers were still convinced of their own culture's superiority, but in fact they had been overtaken technologically by advances in the West. The gap became glaringly apparent in the mid-nineteenth century, when China was humiliatingly defeated in two wars fought by the commercially minded British defending their free-market right to sell opium into China (business that paid for Britain's imports of Chinese tea, porcelain and silk) despite government attempts to ban the trade.

Peasant uprisings and natural disasters also contributed to a catalogue of calamities that finally led to the overthrow of the Qing dynasty and the end of more than two millennia of imperial rule in 1912. Once more in its history, China was divided up between competing warlords. Invasion by Japanese armies complicated the internal anarchy, creating a time of bloodshed and confusion that came to an end only when Mao Ze Dong succeeded in imposing a totalitarian regime in 1949.

Following Communist orthodoxy, Mao set about eliminating religious influence as a relic of the feudal past. Throughout China, churches and monasteries were closed down. Confucianism too came under attack – Mao himself confessed that he had hated the sage from childhood. In the rage for modernization and progress, even ancient family traditions came under fire; ancestor worship finally lost its grip, and the custom of burning paper money, clothes and furniture at funerals to provide the deceased with symbolic belongings for the afterlife was officially encouraged to end.

Yet history casts a long shadow in China, and even under Mao's rationalist rule echoes of old beliefs could still occasionally be heard. At the height of the Cultural Revolution of the 1960s, students greeted their leader with the cry "Ten thousand years to Chairman Mao" – a salute harking back to the impossibly long-lived emperors of the nation's legendary past. Ten years later the people of Beijing showed their respect for the deceased moderate leader Zhou Enlai and their distaste for his enemies, the radical Gang of Four, by laying out thousands of white wreaths in his memory during the Qing Ming festival, traditionally the time for honoring dead kinfolk.

Despite the huge changes that have taken place there over the past fifty years, it is now clear that China's mythology is too deeply ingrained in the national consciousness to be easily expunged.

An early 19th-century portrait of an unnamed empress, her imperial robes decorated with dragons and a phoenix. During the 20th century China may have rid itself of its ancient dynastic tradition but much of its culture and mythology remains intact.

THE TOTALITY OF FIVE

Five appears recurrently in Chinese mythology and culture as a form of classification and an important symbol of totality. The Chinese conceived of the world as consisting of the four geographical directions plus the center, where China (the Middle Kingdom) itself lay. Each of these five directions was represented by a god, a color, a mountain and one of the Five Elements (see page 19). In addition, the Chinese list Five Emperors, Five Excellences, Five Tastes, Five Tones, Five Clouds, Five Precepts, Five Grains, the Five Classics of the Confucian canon, as well as Five Blessings, Five Virtues, Five Classes of Spiritual Beings and Five Beasts for Sacrifice. It might not be coincidental that in the Luo Shu, which inspired Fu Xi, the numbers one to nine are arranged in a magic square so that in any direction they add up to fifteen, and the number at the center is five.

Five Blessings: Long Life, Wealth, Peace, Virtue, Fame.

Right: **A 19th-century vase decorated with four old men. Age is accorded great respect in Chinese culture, where ancestors are revered. Age is associated with experience and wisdom, both positive attributes.**

Five Virtues: Piety, Uprightness, Manners, Knowledge, Trust.

Above: **Confucian philosophy emphasized learning and education. The master stressed that people should look to the past to deepen their understanding of how to behave. The Five Classics were the basis of training for state officials and bureaucrats who advanced through five different levels.**

䷷ Five Classics: Books of Changes, History, Poetry, Rites, and Spring-Autumn Annals.

Left: The sacred Yi Jing (seen here in a 10th-century edition) was consulted by ancient rulers who threw yarrow stalks in order to construct hexagrams for divinatory purposes.

䷸ Five Directions: South, West, North, East, Center.

Right: This bronze, 8th-century marriage mirror belonged at one time to Emperor Hui Zong. It is decorated with five sacred mountains in each direction, the central one representing Kunlun. The mountains for the four directions are lapped by waves from the four seas and the beaded round border is the circle of Heaven.

䷿ Five Beasts for Sacrifice: Ox, Sheep, Dog, Fowl, Pig.

Below: A sheep and a goat by the 13th-century artist Zhao Mengfu, better known as a painter of horses. The word for sheep, Yang, also means ram or goat.

QUESTIONS OF HEAVEN

The anonymous text *Questions of Heaven*, compiled in around the fourth century BCE, takes the form of a set of questions about a group of ancient myths. But no one has ever found an earlier, original account of the myths themselves, which had to be reconstructed from the fourth-century text during the Han dynasty (206 BCE–220 CE). This round-about mode of transmission is typical of the way in which Chinese mythology has been passed down to us.

Nearly all the stories that follow in this chapter draw on the most ancient myths, from a time before writing. They are inconsistent with one another, having developed in different parts of the huge area that was to become China. Their original form is further obscured by the fact that the earliest written versions have nearly all disappeared, many no doubt lost in the Burning of the Books in 213 BCE (see page 18). What we have are either fragments of the stories as reflected in illustrative anecdotes in the surviving works of the early philosophers, or later reconstructions dating from the Han dynasty.

The reconstructions were assembled by scholars brought up in the humanistic Confucian tradition, with a taste for order and balance. They took the mass of formless myth and imposed on it the image of the China they knew. New gods – from Daoism and, later, from Buddhism – to a large extent took the place of old ones, and the early gods, who were authority figures, therefore became equated with emperors, already regarded as semi-divine "Sons of Heaven." Like their Earthly counterparts the gods were ordered neatly into dynasties, though different authorities gave different lineages. This pseudo-historical bias is an unusual characteristic of Chinese mythology because the contents of many of the myths themselves resemble others from India or central Asia. For example, the story of Pan Gu, Creator of the universe, may have been brought by Buddhist travellers from Tibet. This tale superseded older ones featuring the creator goddess Nü Wa (often pronounced Nü Gua) that probably hark back to a time when the feminine was regarded as the life-giving force. As happened to so many ancient goddesses, Nü Wa was married off by later mythmakers to a culture-hero, Fu Xi, who eventually became more powerful than his consort. This series of myths concludes with the gifts of Shen Nong, Fu Xi's successor.

Above: **This 7th-century piece of pottery is a tomb guardian and is said to resemble the mythical beasts guarding the entrance to the Western Paradise known as Kunlun.**

Opposite: *Flying Snow on Myriad Peaks*, **a silk scroll by the 17th-century artist Lan Ying. Chinese mythology recognized four cardinal mountains set out in a square frame, the most significant pattern in traditional thought.**

From the Vapors of Chaos

In Chinese mythology, the act of creation was understood as a matter not of bringing something out of nothing, but of turning formlessness into an ordered pattern. The universe came into being when existing elements, previously mingled in chaos, were set apart in an arranged fashion. The ancient Chinese imagined the primeval chaos as a cloud of moist vapor, suspended in darkness.

In one account there was no creator as such, simply a mysterious coming into being. According to this version, before the beginning of time everything was contained in the vast cloud of moisture; all was one, until the act of ordering transformed the unity of chaos into the duality of opposites: yin and yang (see box opposite), Heaven and Earth, light and darkness. Then the interaction of opposites led to the variety and multiplicity of the universe.

In another account, from the *Huai Nan Zi* text of the mid-second century BCE, two nameless gods were said to have emerged from chaos and then made the sky and Earth. The gods were so immense, stretching from the lowest depths to the utmost heights, that their size was beyond any human comprehension. The pair divided into the elements yin and yang and gave form to hardness and softness as well as the variety of all living things found in the universe.

The most commonly told tale, however, was that of Pan Gu, a late addition to the body of Chinese myth that some scholars date to the third century CE and others to the following century. It assumed great importance and came to overshadow earlier creation myths featuring the mother goddess Nü Wa (see pages 38–41). The concept of a cosmic egg and the transformation of a primordial man into the natural features of the universe are also found in Hindu mythology, and many scholars argue that the Pan Gu myth was probably influenced by tales from central Asia.

The story of Pan Gu tells how, before Heaven and Earth were separated, there was chaos – vast and unknowable – containing all the elements of creation. It took the form of moist darkness within a giant egg. At its heart Pan Gu, the Creator, slowly came to life. For 18,000 years Pan Gu slumbered in the midst of formlessness, growing all the time. Finally, he awoke. He had the shape of a stout man, short in stature but with strong arms and shoulders; in one hand he held a chisel and in the other an axe. In the darkness he flailed about him with these tools, splitting

The legend of Pan Gu provides the first comprehensive Chinese account of the origin of all things. Some believe it to have been devised by the Daoist Ge Hong in the 4th century CE to give accessible form to abstract philosophical accounts of universal order. This 19th-century illustration shows Pan Gu holding the egg of chaos composed of the intertwined symbols of yin and yang.

Yin and Yang

Pan Gu's creative power separated the elements into yin and yang, Earth and Heaven. In traditional Chinese thought these opposing but complementary forces are believed to permeate not just all life but the entire universe.

Yin is associated with female, absorbing qualities: passivity, darkness and the moon. Yang is linked to male, penetrating qualities: activity, brightness and the sun. In the realm of beasts, yin is the tiger and yang the dragon; in the landscape, valleys are yin and mountains yang. A broken line and even numbers are yin, an unbroken line and odd numbers are yang. Throughout the universe the two qualities are in constant fluctuation – one giving way as the other expands, so that, for example, light gives way to dark, heat to cold, and vice versa. Their interaction is understood to be the very process of life, and yin and yang are shown together as the dark and light surfaces of a circle.

The first development of the concept is lost to history but by the third century BCE Daoist philosphers – led by Zou Yan – were presenting yin-yang as a theory of everything underlying history and cosmology. Zou Yan is traditionally also credited with developing the notion of the Wu Xing, or Five Elements – earth, wood, metal, fire and water – that were linked to yin-yang. This proposed that history and the universe were patterned by the interactions of the agents and that these were themselves aspects of the yin-yang fluctuation.

In Daoist thought the yin-yang opposition is a manifestation of the transcendent unity of Dao (the "Way" – see page 17). Daoism also associates yin and yang with the two souls possessed by each individual – the material soul (yin) and the heavenly soul named hun (yang). When the two were united, a person would enjoy good health, but conflict or division between the two resulted in illness or perhaps even death.

This amulet shows a tiger (the king of beasts and identified with the west) below a circle representing yin and yang, the opposing and complementary principles of the universe. The eight trigrams, or Ba gua, depicted around the circle are the key to knowledge, having been invented by Fu Xi, the first of the Three Sovereigns.

the egg open and sending the elements of creation flying through space. The lighter, purer parts, or yang, flew upward and became Heaven, while the heavier ones, or yin, sank to take shape as the Earth. In one place Heaven and Earth were linked but Pan Gu worked away at the join until they were separated.

The creation myths tell how various parts of Pan Gu's body became magically transformed into the five sacred mountains that are such a central part of Chinese mythology. These peaks were the source of all power and were also associated with the Five Elements. The pine-clad hillsides seen here are the Huangshan ("Yellow") Mountains in the province of Anhui.

Pan Gu stood with his feet on the Earth and the sky resting on his head. He found that the yin and yang elements continued moving apart with the force of the blows he had struck. Every day the sky grew higher by one *zhang* (three meters) and the Earth grew one *zhang* thicker; Pan Gu increased in size at the same rate. For another period of 18,000 years he resolutely kept his place, for he feared that if he did not keep them apart sky and Earth would fall back into each other's embrace and order would collapse into chaos. By the end of this time Pan Gu was vast almost beyond imagining, stretching like an endless pillar from the ground to the furthest reaches of the sky.

Eventually Pan Gu could see that his task of separation was done. Exhausted by his toils, he lay down upon the Earth and died – and his vast body was transformed. When alive his virile action had brought order and difference out of chaotic unity, and in death he gave the plain Earth a wealth of new and beautiful forms. His breath became the winds, his voice the blast of thunder, his left eye the sun and his right eye the moon, his bristling hair and beard the glittering stars of the night sky and his sweat the rains. His hands and feet became the four corners of the square Earth, and his body the five sacred mountains that were homes to the gods (see pages 34–37). His lifeblood became the rivers and streams that water the Earth, his flesh was the fields, his body hair the grass and slender trees, his teeth and bones minerals and rocks, his semen and bone marrow precious pearls and jade. The fleas on his body transformed into the human race.

In some myths, Pan Gu controlled the weather, bringing sunshine when he was happy and storms when he was angry or sad. Despite the fact that he grew to such a size, images of Pan Gu show him as a dwarf wearing a bearskin or a dress of leaves, often with a horned head and holding the chisel and axe that he used for the creation. In some earlier versions of the myth, his head became the Eastern Mountain, his feet the Western Mountain, his left hand the Southern Mountain, his right hand the Northern Mountain and his stomach the Mountain of the Center.

Allegory of the End of Chaos

An alternative allegorical account of the creation of order from chaos was given in the fourth century BCE by the philosopher Zhuangzi. According to this version, the Emperor of the Southern Sea, Shu, and

A clothes pin that dates from the early part of the Qing dynasty and consists of two jade bi disks entwined with ferocious looking dragons. According to myth, jade is derived from the bone marrow of Pan Gu; and the material is considered by the Chinese to have magical and curative properties. Bi is the symbol for the circular sky or Heaven and the hole at the center corresponds to the lie kou through which the lightning flashes. The bi was used ritually by the king who had bestowed on him by Heaven the mandate to rule on Earth provided that he remained virtuous – hence the title "Son of Heaven."

the Emperor of the Northern Sea, Hu, often met to discuss and compare their realms. Each was willing to travel halfway to encounter the other and they met in the land of the Emperor of the Center, Hun-tun ("Chaos").

Hun-tun always made the other emperors most welcome and attended to all their needs while they were visiting him. But he suffered because he did not have the seven holes that humans have in their heads – and so could not breathe, see, hear or eat. The emperors Shu and Hu wanted to make a gift to Hun-tun because he was so attentive and generous to them, and suggested that they would make the holes in him to improve the quality of his life. Hun-tun accepted their offer happily, so Shu and Hu set to work. Each day they drilled one hole in Hun-tun's head; for the first six days, all went well, but while they were drilling the seventh and final hole Hun-tun died. In that moment, the universe was born.

The two emperors' names combined, *shu-hu*, mean lightning and, clearly, one interpretation of the allegory is that it was the electrical energy of lightning that transformed chaos. In traditional Chinese cosmogony there was said to be a hole in the top of the sky named *lie kou*, and through this aperture lightning sent its fiery darts. Hun-tun was sometimes thought of as a bird, and owls, in particular, were associated with chaos.

The Square Earth

The ancient Chinese believed that the Earth was square and unmoving, surrounded by seas on all four sides and overarched by a circular, turning sky. The life-giving rain that fell on the land ran off into the seas.

According to one cosmology known to predate the Qin era (221–207 BCE), the sky was like an upturned bowl, circling around the still point of the Pole Star. When Gong Gong (Spirit of the Waters) blundered into the Buzhou Mountain (see page 40), he not only made a hole in the firmament but also caused the whole sky to tip so that the Pole Star was no longer in its center. The square Earth was yin and the circular sky was yang. The structure of the universe was often likened to that of the Chinese chariot, which had a square carriage beneath a circular umbrella; however, while the chariot umbrella stood on a central pole, the sky was usually said to be upheld by four – sometimes eight – mountains or pillars.

An alternative cosmology proposed that the universe was like a vast egg standing on end: the Earth floated on a great ocean, filling the bottom of the shell, and the stars and planets moved across the inner shell that arched overhead.

The Chinese dragon – seen here in a 16th-century frieze – was a benevolent creature embodying wisdom and strength. The First Emperor chose it as his imperial emblem.

Within the real landscape lay a mythical one with five sacred mountains – one for each point of the compass and a fifth in the center. Each of the cardinal directions was linked to an animal, a season and an elemental force (see the boxes on pages 19 and 31). East was associated with the Green Dragon, the season of spring and the element of wood; west with the White Tiger, autumn and metal; south with the Red Phoenix, summer and fire; and north with a black tortoise-snake hybrid named the Dark Warrior, winter and water. The fifth point, the center, identified with China itself, was associated with the color yellow and the element of earth.

It is said that the north was feared in earliest times and was not worshipped, but the emperors of the Han dynasty (206 BCE–220 CE) claimed to hold power under its protection and made sacrifices and devotions in that direction.

The two mountains of the east and the west were particularly important. The Eastern Mountain, Taishan, was near Qufu in northeastern China. From the second century BCE on, Taishan was widely believed to rise above an underworld

Heavenly Bodies

Ten suns and twelve moons lived at the eastern and western edges of the Earth, taking it in turns to cast light on the toils of women and men. The watery moons were yin, the fiery suns yang.

At the far east of the square Earth ten bright suns existed in the Valley of Light, where they were cared for by their gentle mother. Near the valley's edge was a lake on whose banks a hollow mulberry tree towered high in the heavens. Each morning the suns' mother washed them in the lake, then the sun whose turn it was to cross the sky climbed to the top of the tree while the other nine followed as far as the lower branches. The chosen sun rode across the heavens in a chariot controlled by its mother and hauled by strong dragons. At the end of the day, in the far west, the sun found another vast tree and returned to Earth by way of its branches. Red flowers covered the western tree and shone softly in the near dark, casting a glow across the evening sky; some people said these were the stars.

Like the suns, the twelve moons – one for each month – were cared for by their mother. They lived in a lake at the Earth's western edge and took similar turns to travel in the chariot.

A moonlit evening depicted with some classic elements of Chinese art, including mountains, trees and water.

where souls resided after death. Only great rulers were able to perform religious sacrifices on this peak. Chroniclers of the Han era set out to glorify their own emperor by telling how the Qin ruler Shi Huangdi tried and failed to perform a sacrifice there because bad weather, presumably controlled by the wind god, drove him to the lower slopes.

Sacrifices on the five mountains were a way of demonstrating wide dominion and a dynasty's right to rule. A body of stories grew up in which ores from the mountains were used for making dynastic swords. The smith became a mysterious figure and his handiwork was imbued with magical power, a little of which was thought to go into each weapon.

One such tale was told of the King of Wu near the mouth of the Yangtzi River. He ordered two grand swords from a smith named Gan Jiang.

The Three Sovereigns

The mythical history of ancient China recounts that after the death of Pan Gu, the land was governed by three rulers in turn, the last of whom ushered in the "Ten Epochs" during which men and women learned essential skills, including hunting and farming.

The first of the three rulers was the sinuous Lord of Heaven, who took the form of a great serpent with the feet of a wild animal and lived in the Kunlun Mountains in northwest China. He was a mighty creature with twelve heads who reigned for 18,000 years. His successor, the Lord of Earth, had an identical appearance and ruled for the same length of time, but he took up residence in the Dragon Gate Mountains (thought to be peaks in Henan Province). The third

was the Lord of Man, who settled in a place named Xing Ma (probably in modern Sichuan). He presided over the first of the "Ten Epochs" detailed by the ninth-century AD historian Sima Zhen, who based his work on very old sources that have since been lost.

Shen Nong (*right*) taught people to plough the land and harvest crops during the Ninth Epoch. With Fu Xi, he was reinvented during the Han period as a "historical" ruler.

The smith set off with his pregnant wife Mo Ye, and travelled far and wide in the Five Mountains to find suitable ores. After he had gathered the minerals, he carefully plotted a propitious time to cast the swords – when yin and yang would be in conjunction. But he found that no matter how well he planned, no matter how expertly he prepared his furnace and heated the ore, the material would not give up its metal.

He told Mo Ye that many years earlier, when faced with a similar problem, his old master and the master's wife had flung themselves into the flames, and two superb swords had been the result. Inspired by this, Mo Ye threw pieces of her hair and clippings from her nails into the furnace and Gan Jiang cast two wonderful swords, a male one that he named after himself and a female one he named after his wife.

He hid the male sword and gave the female one to the king but the king discovered the deception and slaughtered Gan Jiang. Just before he

expired, however, the smith told Mo Ye that their child would grow up to avenge him – and it came to pass as he had predicted. The son cut his own head off with the sword named after his father; a stranger took it to the king, who threw the head into a furnace and when it would not melt was persuaded by the stranger to cut off his own head; this was cast into the flames and then the stranger decapitated himself, his head fell into the furnace and the three human heads solidified into a single piece of metal with marvellous properties. In some versions of the tale, Mo Ye also hurled herself into the furnace – presumably after giving birth – to enable the swords to be made.

In the far west lay the towering Kunlun Mountain, where four rivers rose to water the four quarters of the land; and in the east, at Guixu far out in the Eastern Sea, lay five holy mountains that were home to the immortals. Kunlun was a mythical peak but was associated with the actual Kunlun range. In some versions those who found

Kunlun and drank the vivid red waters that flowed from it became immortal. As the source of life-giving waters, Kunlun Mountain is very similar to the Hindus' Mount Meru – and the two are often linked by scholars.

Kunlun stretched from Earth to sky, and downward beneath the Earth's surface for the same distance. It rose through nine levels and from doors in its sides the winds blew. The east-facing door of light was guarded by a fabulous creature with nine human heads and the body of a fierce tiger. The Lord of the Sky made his home there, and the birds of Kunlun did his bidding.

The majestic palace of Xi Wang Mu, Queen Mother of the West (see pages 78–79), was located on Kunlun's wonderful slopes, and the mountain was also home to the Lord of the Rain, usually seen as an armor-clad warrior who used a sword to flick water onto the needy Earth. In a tale told of Shen Nong (see page 46), the Lord of the Rain used a branch to sprinkle water and save the world from a terrible drought ushered in by the god of the burning wind. One story cast the Lord of the Rain as the chrysalis of a silkworm accompanied by a magical long-legged bird. The bird appeared at the court of Qi and danced before the courtiers on one leg; when the prince sent to Confucius asking what the sighting could mean, the wise one said it was a sign of coming rain. In the storms that followed Qi was the only state not to be flooded.

Kunlun was said to be the source of the great Yellow River. Its presiding god was He Bo, known as the Count of the River, once a mortal man who had tied stones to his back and thrown himself into its waters, thereby gaining immortality and wonderful powers. His cult centered on annual sacrifices held at Ye and Linjin. For many years until the end of the Zhou era (1030–221 BCE), a young woman was each year offered as bride to the Count of the River. After celebrations and ritual preparations, she was tied to a marriage bed and sent to her death on the gushing waters. After human sacrifice had ended, travellers who could afford it made offerings of precious jade ornaments to He Bo before venturing onto the river.

This boulder of jade is 40 cm high and has been deeply carved on both sides in the form of Red Cliff, an idyllic mountain, cleft by rushing waterfalls, its ledges dotted with pagodas and pines.

37

Mother of the World

Mother deity Nü Wa was called to save the Earth and its people when the sky threatened to fall in after a dispute among the gods. She appeared in many guises, sometimes as a beautiful goddess or a child, at others as a human-headed serpent. Fu Xi, her brother or husband, accompanied her in later versions of the myths.

In a tale from the Han dynasty (206 BCE–220 CE) Nü Wa created the first human beings. According to this account, after Earth and Heaven had come into being, Nü Wa roamed the land. The sky was filled with stars and the waters with fish, while the fertile countryside was teeming with animals – but Nü Wa felt lonely. Pausing at a pond, she looked into the waters, saw her own reflection and thought sadly how much pleasure a few companions would give her. Then it struck the goddess that she could use her divine powers to create companions in her own likeness.

Stooping low, Nü Wa took a handful of mud from the water's edge and began to mold it into shape, fashioning a tiny body with two arms and two legs. As soon as she set it down, it took life and capered on the grass before her. Nü Wa was pleased with the being she had created and set to work to make more. The creatures she made were the first people.

Nü Wa labored until the sun in its chariot drawn by dragons had finished its journey across Heaven and the night sky was sparkling with stars; then she rested, laying her head on a rock. In the morning she carried on as before. The goddess

Creator goddess Nü Wa and her husband Fu Xi are depicted coiled around one another in this Chinese silk funerary banner, which dates from the 6th or 7th century CE; their yin-yang partnership re-established cosmic harmony. The wings are indicative of immortality.

made scores of little people, desiring to fill the Earth with the creatures, but it was slow work. After some time she paused, looking about at the towering mountains and endless plains, and understood that at the rate she was going she would never be able to make enough humans to fill the Earth. So she took a rope or builder's cord, dipped it into the mud and swung it about her so that drops of mud fell on the ground all around. As the clods landed they turned into more people like those she had so laboriously molded with her hands. In this ingenious way Nü Wa made countless humans, enough to populate the Earth in all its vastness.

Pan Gu Creates the First People

An alternative account of the first days combines the myths of Pan Gu and Nü Wa, claiming that Pan Gu himself made the first people out of clay.

The Creator Pan Gu separated Heaven and Earth, and then brought plants and animals into being. But he felt unhappy with his handiwork, because none of the birds and beasts had the power of reason; he decided there ought to be one creature with the ability to care for and make use of other living beings.

With his strong, skillful hands he began to mold the first people from mud, and as he finished each figure he set it to dry in the sunshine. Some of the creatures he filled with the female qualities of yin and fashioned into women, others he endowed with the male qualities of yang, turning them into men. He worked all day beneath the hot sun, piling up his people against a rock outcrop.

As the sun went down he straightened his aching back and looked up at the sky, where he saw a bank of dark stormclouds. Some of the clay people had not yet dried and he realized that his handiwork would be obliterated if the storm broke over the figures. He hurried to move them into the shelter of a nearby cave, but as he worked a great wind arose, whipping up the clouds until they filled the sky. Pan Gu cried aloud with anguish as the thunder cracked and the rains poured down while he was still moving the figures. Those damaged were the ancestors of people with unusually shaped bodies or disabilities.

The phoenix, or feng huang, indicated happiness and luck – a sign of Heaven's favor. Just as the dragon was identified with yang and the emperor, so the phoenix was associated with yin and the empress. The phoenix was the symbol for the cardinal direction of south – often being referred to as The Red Bird of the South – and represented drought, the element fire and the season summer.

According to many versions of the myth, the people Nü Wa made by hand were aristocrats and rulers, while those she flicked from her twirling rope became the "black-haired," a common name for peasants. The rope was sometimes said to be a reed or vine she had plucked from the bank beside the pond. The goddess was usually depicted as a human-headed dragon or snake, so clearly she did not create humans exactly in her own image. She was also said to have taught her creatures to marry and breed, for she realized that if she had to replace all the humans who died her creative task would be without end.

For many years Nü Wa's creatures lived a happy life, watching their children and grandchildren grow to maturity, but then calamity struck. The overarching sky was damaged following a bitter dispute among the gods.

In some accounts the quarrel was between Gong Gong, Spirit of the Water, and Jurong, Spirit of Fire. They fought in the far north of the country at the foot of Buzhou Mountain, a mythical peak that, according to the tales, lay northwest of the Kunlun Mountains and was one of the pillars that held the sky in position. Gong Gong sent floodwaters but they were driven back by Jurong's ravenous fires. This defeat drove Gong Gong wild with rage. He blundered into Buzhou Mountain like a maddened boar, reducing it to rubble.

Without the mountain peak to support it, the northern sky tilted toward the ground. Half the sky tumbled in, and great cracks opened up in the Earth; the sun, moon and stars fell into the path that is familiar today. Waters poured out of the chasms in the ground, covering the plains, but on higher land, flames ravaged the forests. As a consequence of the shuddering impact, the northwest reared up and ever afterward rivers and streams ran away to the southeast where they gathered to form the seas, found there to this day. Maddened by fear, wild beasts rampaged far and wide, attacking and devouring the fleeing people, while sharp-beaked birds desperate for food swept down from the skies to peck the last flesh off the bones of corpses. The seasons fell out of their proper order.

Nü Wa Repairs the Damaged Heavens

Nü Wa acted swiftly to repair the damage caused by Gong Gong. First she took some boulders from a river swollen with floodwaters and set a fire so fierce that it melted the stones to a thick liquid. She used this as a paste to patch the pieces of the ravaged sky back together. Next the goddess looked around for something to support the heavens and stop them falling in again, and her gaze fell on a tortoise. She took the beast, sliced off its four legs and erected them as supports for the sky at the four corners of the square Earth (see pages 34–37). She drove away the fierce beasts that had been preying on people, especially a black-skinned dragon that patrolled the Yellow River valley, whipping up floods. She controlled the floodwaters by building dikes made from the ashes of burned reeds.

Nü Wa's work was done. Order returned to the universe, and a new era of comfort was ushered in for her people. Wild animals lived peaceably alongside humans, and food crops grew quickly in the fertile soil. Nü Wa was delighted and, according to some myths, she rewarded the survivors with the first musical instrument, a thirteen-piped instrument named the *shenghuang*; in most accounts, however, it was Fu Xi who taught people how to make music (see page 43). Content at last, she laid herself down to die and, as with Pan Gu (see page 33), new wonders emerged from her dead body. In one account, ten gods sprang from her intestines and took up position as guards of the land of mortals.

There are many versions of the linked myths of Nü Wa and Gong Gong. In some, the skies fell in – for unknown reasons – and Nü Wa repaired the heavens long before Gong Gong came to Earth and caused further damage. Sometimes Gong Gong, rather than fighting the fire god, was said to have led a revolt against the mythical Emperor Zhuan Xu – ruler of gods and men who reigned from 2513 BCE to 2435 BCE. Some scholars identify Nü Wa as an

ancient mother deity; certainly her myth predates that of Pan Gu by several centuries. She is mentioned in texts of the fourth century BCE, some 700 years before Pan Gu made his first appearance.

The myth of the toppling sky and the rearing Earth explains the topography of China, accounting for the fact that mountains rise in the northwest and there are flat, river-fed plains in the southeast. Another version of the same story, told in the *Classic of Mountains and Seas* (c.400 BCE–100 CE), used the tale to explain the creation of day, night and the seasons. According to this account, after Gong Gong's collision with the mountain had torn a hole in the northwestern sky, the sun's place was taken by a red-skinned dragon with a human head. When the dragon breathed out it was winter and when it breathed in summer reigned. If its eyes were open, it was day, but when it closed them night fell. Its breath was also responsible for the wind.

The tortoise was a familiar symbol of stability for the ancient Chinese. The animal also had sacred associations: its shell was used in divination rites and its four legs were used as pillars by Nü Wa to prop up Heaven, thus establishing it as a link between Heaven and Earth. This bronze dates from the Han dynasty (206 BCE–220 CE) and is inlaid with gold and silver.

41

The Great Flood

In later myths Nü Wa's role as great mother was modified to allow for a masculine contribution to the origin of people. According to one tale derived from the myths of the southern Yao and Miao peoples, Nü Wa and Fu Xi (sometimes called Brother and Sister Fu Xi) were peasant children who married to produce a new race of humans.

On a stormy day dragon-bodied Thunder himself came down to Earth and was captured and caged by the peasant father of a boy and a girl. His crops ruined, the peasant decided to serve Thunder up as a meal. He needed to go out to market but told the children they would be quite safe as long as Thunder was not given any water. But while he was gone the girl became concerned by Thunder's groans and flicked a little water into his mouth. Thunder shouted for joy, then burst out of the cage with a terrible bang.

Thunder gave the children a fang from his mouth, telling them to bury it and harvest the plant that grew from it. When the peasant returned and saw what had happened he set to work building an iron ship – for he guessed that a great flood was on its way.

Meanwhile the planted tooth grew in a single day into a vine that produced a giant calabash, a kind of gourd. The children sliced off the top and found rows and rows of sharp teeth like the one they had used as a seed. They pulled them out and created a small, soft sailing boat with room for both the girl and her brother. The storm then broke and the peasant jumped into his boat and

This 9th-century Buddhist painted silk depicts a thunder-bearer. A Tang-dynasty piece, it is from an important collection of such works found in caves in the Valley of the Thousand Buddhas at the Chinese end of the Silk Road.

his children clambered into the calabash as the floodwaters rose. Little by little the mountain peaks disappeared and before too long the boats had risen so high that they reached the Ninth Heaven, abode of the gods. The peasant knocked at the gates of Heaven to demand entry, angering the Spirit of the Waters, Gong Gong, so much that he forced the flood to retreat with such speed that the calabash and boat hurtled downward. The soft calabash bounced safely, but the iron boat shattered on impact, killing the peasant.

The two children were alone in the world, for all the other people had drowned. Yet they learned how to survive by planting and growing food. Because the soft fruit had saved them, they took the name Fu Xi, from the word for calabash, calling themselves Brother and Sister Fu Xi.

Eventually they married and in due course Sister Fu Xi became pregnant and produced a meatball from her womb. They chopped the strange object into many pieces and wrapped it in paper, but a sudden gust of wind swept it away and scattered the fragments, which fell to the earth where they took form as humans. A new race grew up to people the Earth.

Fu Xi Scales the Heavenly Ladder

One account of Fu Xi's life made him the son of a country maiden and the god of thunder. He had a divine nature and could come and go between Earth and Heaven on the tree of Jianmu that linked the two realms.

The mythical territory of Huaxu was an Earthly paradise where people lived to a very great age. They enjoyed a blessed life without fear of fire or water and could follow the invisible paths of the sky as if they were roaming on the ground. A maiden of this land was one day wandering through the swamp of Leize, when she came across a giant's vast footprints in the soft ground. Curious, she stepped into the indentation, which was the footprint of the god of thunder. She felt strangely warmed in her belly and later discovered she was pregnant. In due course she gave birth to a healthy boy, whom she named Fu Xi.

The child had the nature and attributes of a god, and he could come and go between Earth and the heavenly realm. He went by way of the tree of Jianmu that grew at the very center of the Duguang plain in southwest China. It had long and tangled roots, but above ground grew straight up without branches for miles into the sky. No mortal could find a grip on the smooth, soft bark. At the very top, far above the Earth, there was a proliferation of branches.

The plain of Duguang where the tree of Jianmu grew was said to be the very center of the Earth and was itself a paradise – a place where plants and trees never dropped their leaves and a wonderful and diverse menagerie of beasts and birds had assembled.

Fu Xi, traveller between Heaven and Earth, taught mortal people many wonderful things. Among other things, he showed them how to make fire by rubbing sticks together, and how to use it for cooking. He made a stringed instrument and showed men and women how to make music. Inspired by the intricacy and effectiveness of the spider's web, Fu Xi also made a net that people could use for hunting and fishing.

Lin Jun and the Water Goddess

One of Fu Xi's descendants, Lin Jun, won Earthly fame as leader of an exodus of five tribes from their rugged Zhongli Mountain home in southern China. During a long river journey his heroic bearing and good looks attracted the attention of a beautiful but jealous goddess.

The tribes scratched a living on the rocky slopes, having learned to live peacefully with one another under Lin Jun, who had triumphed in a trial of skill and strength held to decide their leader.

Over the years – since war no longer ravaged the population – their numbers grew and grew, and it became ever harder to produce enough food to survive. Lin Jun decided that they must find a new home, so they set out along the Yi River (now called the Luohe, in Henan Province). After a week of the trek Lin Jun called a stop at Yanyang where a tributary joined the river.

The tribes put up their tents next to the river. On the first evening, as Lin Jun took a walk along the bank, he encountered a beautiful maiden, whose long hair was dripping wet as if she had just clambered out of the river. She spoke softly to him, welcoming him and his people to the place and proposing that they should settle there – for there was enough space and good supplies of fish

and salt. She left Lin Jun in no doubt that she was attracted to him. He was captivated by her slender form, but was not convinced that the scrub countryside would be a good place to settle.

That night he lay awake, listening to the waters close by. He heard his tentflap lift and looked up to see the maiden creeping toward his bed. The lovers swooned with delight in each other's embrace; then, as dawn broke, Lin Jun had a rude shock when his partner – actually a river goddess – turned into an insect and flew away. A cloud of other insects came to greet her, all of them really local fairies and elves who took this form only to help her slip away.

On the following nights the goddess returned to dally with her mortal lover, but she could not persuade him to stay. One evening Lin Jun called the tribes together and told them that they had

rested long enough and must leave the following dawn. That night the goddess did not come to Lin Jun, and in the morning the camp was surrounded by a thick cloud of insects.

Lin Jun knew that the goddess was at the heart of the cloud, trying to prevent his departure. He called out to her to let his people go, but there was no reply. Then he thought of a way of identifying her. He sent a messenger to a distant point on the riverbank with a length of green silk thread. He told the man to lay the thread on the ground and announce that Lin Jun had changed his mind and would now stay by the river – if the goddess came to him in her insect form wearing the thread, which was a symbol of his undying love for her.

She did not visit, and the next day they were once more surrounded by insects. But when Lin Jun peered into the cloud, he could see the green thread floating near its center. He seized a bow and arrow and at once took aim at the thread; when he loosed the arrow there was a brilliant flash and a shrill whistle – and the goddess became visible, with the arrow through her heart.

She fell into the salt water and floated silently away; all the other insects disappeared and the sun was again visible. Released from the insect plague, the people capered and danced with joy around Lin Jun, but he stood gloomily staring at the disappearing goddess. He threw away his bow and arrows, frightened by what he had done.

The tribes set off immediately and after some days they came to a gloomy place. Lin Jun's spirits were low. But then the riverbank split open to reveal a staircase. Some brave souls climbed it. At the top they gasped with wonder, for they saw a wide, sundrenched plain rich with life. When Lin Jun threw some lengths of bamboo onto a large, flat stone they stuck there, as if growing – and he declared this to be a sign that the spot was blessed by his ancestor Fu Xi. The five tribes settled in this new land and built a wonderful city named Yi.

Guangxi's towering peaks appear to collide with Heaven itself. Mountains featured often in the myths as home to various gods.

Master of the Harvest

Ancient peoples, having been taught how to hunt and fish by Fu Xi during the Ninth Epoch, learned the skills needed for a more settled way of life from his successor Shen Nong, the Lord of Earth, who taught people how to plough and harvest in the same era.

When Shen Nong was born on Earth, nine wells surrounded his place of birth. They were all fed from one spring, so if water was drawn from any one it affected the levels in all the others. In this era there were many people in China and they struggled to find enough food to meet their needs, surviving by eating plants, fruits, insects, shellfish – whatever came to hand. Shen Nong was inspired to teach people how to plough the land, sow seeds and harvest plentiful food crops. He showed them the qualities of different soils, that some were fertile and that others were barren. They hailed him as the god of agriculture.

Images of the deity show him with a human body and a bull's head, associating him with the ox that pulled the farmer's plow. The ox was originally a star divinity who was dispatched by the Emperor of Heaven to reassure people on Earth that if they worked hard there would always be enough food to eat. But the deity made a mistake in delivering the message – and as a punishment was outlawed from the heavens and required to stay on Earth to help farmers.

An early 15th-century water buffalo carved out of green jade. Shen Nong is often depicted with a bull's head, linking him to fertility.

Gift of the Five Grains

One day as Shen Nong was demonstrating how to plough and plant, a bank of sandy brown clouds appeared and unleashed a storm of seeds. After the clouds had passed, Shen Nong gathered the seeds and carefully planted them. Months later a rich and varied crop covered the fertile land in all directions. The seeds he gave to humans were said to be the Five Grains – traditionally, barley, two types of millet, hemp, and vegetables such as peas and beans. On another occasion when he was instructing the black-haired peasants, a remarkable red bird flew across the plain, carrying in its beak a nine-eared plant that shed seeds as it went. Shen Nong ran about collecting the seeds and then planted them. The plants that subsequently grew from them had marvellous powers to heal and banish hunger and death.

Shen Nong also appeared as god of the fiery wind. Some scholars suggest that in this role he may have been linked with the primitive technique of preparing land by burning vegetation prior to planting seeds in the ash-rich soil. When this was superseded by more settled farming methods such as plowing, the deity took on the attributes of a god of agriculture. One myth tells how during the fiery god's rule as emperor, there was a terrible drought and humankind was saved by Chi Songzi who took a bowl of water, dipped a small branch in it and flicked water on the ground, thereby magically summoning stormclouds that released a needed deluge. Chi became Lord of the Rain. Another of Shen Nong's achievements is said to have been the conversion of the Eight Diagrams invented by Fu Xi into the sixty-four hexagrams contained in the *Yi Jing* (*Book of Changes*).

How the Sea Defeated Jing Wei

Shen Nong's favorite daughter was the delicate, slender-necked Nü Wa, who shared her name with the great goddess who created the first people at the dawn of time. But to his dismay she drowned in a boating accident and after death she vowed to avenge herself on the sea that had killed her.

Shen Nong's daughter loved the sea and took pleasure in rowing on the deep waters far from land, watching the sea birds swoop through the buffeting winds or skim low over the waves. But one day a squall caught her boat and she was swept overboard and drowned. When she did not return that evening, Shen Nong wailed loudly in the echoing dusk – but for all his divine strength he had no power over death and could not restore his lost one to her former shape.

For her part, Nü Wa was filled with a frenzy of anger toward the cruel sea that had ended her life before its time. Her soul took the form of a white-beaked bird with a many-colored head and red feet. Named Jing Wei, the bird looked like a cross between a crow and an owl. It nested on Fajiu Mountain, a northerly peak also known as Fabao or Luge, in modern Shaanxi Province.

From Fajiu the bird flew to the Eastern Sea carrying a pebble or twig in its white beak – and dropped it into the rolling mass of water. Then the girl's spirit told the waves that she would fill them up with wood and stones and make the great ocean into nothing more than a marsh to prevent it robbing any more young people of their lives. But the sea only laughed, and told her she could never achieve her goal, no matter how hard she might try.

Jing Wei turned her back on the proud water with contempt. She flew back to Fajiu Mountain, picked up another twig and returned to drop it into the sea. From that day on the bird known as the jing wei has labored ceaselessly to fill the sea, but despite its efforts the waves still roll and crash upon the shore.

HEAVENLY PREDICTIONS

The Chinese took an interest in the heavens thousands of years ago, systematically mapping the sky, recording and organizing star groupings, and developing their own large system of constellations. Many of these groupings were based on small numbers of stars in relatively small areas of the celestial sphere, offering intricate designs that, naturally enough, often reflected Chinese life: the emperor, his officials and eunuchs were all represented in the sky and there were four superconstellations symbolizing the four seasons. The patterns observed in the sky helped to establish a sacred topography and confirmed the role of the emperor as the intermediary between the gods in Heaven and mortals on Earth. Astronomy also aided the creation of calendars and the regulation of time, in turn allowing natural cycles to be determined, predictions to be made and auspicious dates to be calculated.

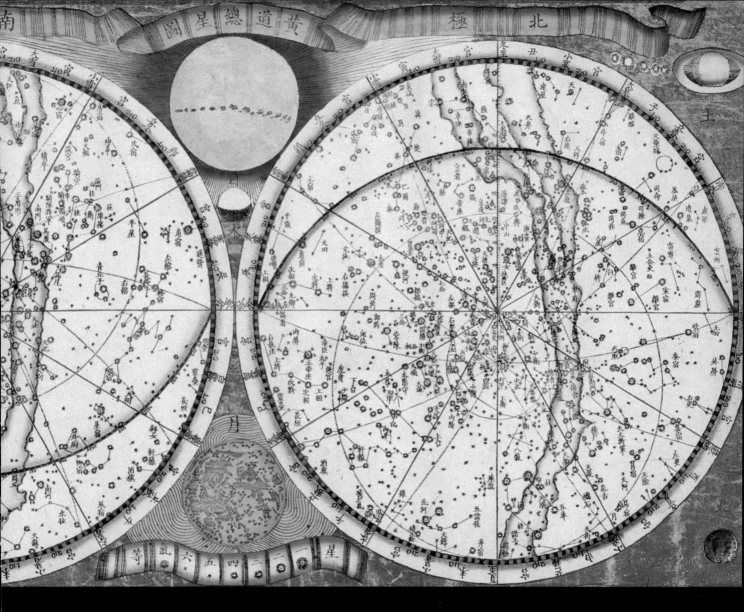

南　　　　黄道總星圖　　　　北極

Far left: This 17th-century lacquer box and cover was a wedding gift. It is decorated with scenes of happiness and good fortune and would originally have contained horoscopes. The Chinese believed that each individual's fortunes were determined by the year, month, day and hour of birth. Prior to any wedding taking place the birth dates of both bride and groom were checked to ensure their compatibility, and the marriage day itself was selected so that it was an auspicious one.

Left: Gold zodiac figure with a rat. As well as being the first animal of the zodiac, the rat is an attendant animal spirit for the Void, one of the 28 lunar mansions or constellations (organized into four groups of seven – one for each season). The Void is the place associated with the tortoise, representing north.

Above: One of the main purposes of Chinese astronomy was to establish and regulate a calendar that governed the agricultural cycle. Such a tool demonstrated the emperor's authority and enabled prior planning. Observers equated the celestial cycles with natural shortages and surpluses; the emperor thus had to try and maintain equilibrium. This late 18th-century sky map on rice paper records 1,464 stars grouped into 283 constellations. The northern celestial sphere is to the right, the southern on the left, with the Milky Way standing out clearly on both.

GIFTS OF THE GODS

During a tour of his territories, the Yellow Emperor, China's greatest mythical sovereign and the legendary ancestor of the Chinese people, visited the eastern coast and encountered a divine creature that understood the secrets of the universe. As the waves thundered upon the shore behind him, the emperor conversed with the deity, named the Beast of the White Marsh, and was instructed in the nature of every living thing. Then the emperor ordered this precious knowledge to be recorded in a chart of the universe, paid homage to the mysterious god and called for the composition of a special prayer.

This resonant tale comes from *Seven Tomes from the Cloudy Shelf* by the Daoist Wang Chuan of the Tang dynasty (618–906 CE). By that time the Yellow Emperor, known as Huang Di, had been revered as the supreme Chinese deity for many centuries. Earlier, in his *Historical Records*, the Han historian Sima Qian (c.145–c.86 BCE) had traced the history of Chinese civilization and established the Yellow Emperor as the great forefather and propagator of Chinese culture. In the Later Han era (25–220 CE), when philosophical Daoism had acquired the characteristics of a religion, Huang Di was adopted as the foremost Daoist god by philosophers keen to lend their beliefs the stamp of antiquity. Sima Qian, and other Han-era writers such as Dai De (author of the *The Elder Dai's Record of Ritual* in the first century BCE), mixed early fragmentary myths with invented material, thus creating "historical" biographies for the early gods, who were thought to have lived at a time when the realms of gods and humans were closer than in their own day. Sima Qian effectively created a new hierarchy of gods, with Huang Di connecting the original Three Sovereigns to the semi-divine, mythical rulers who followed them.

The mythology of China is rich in tales of "culture heroes" – generally deities who taught essential skills or pleasures to humans. In the body of overlapping stories that survive, there are many accounts of their deeds that form a colorful tapestry depicting the development of civilization in China – a pattern made richer still by the people's stories that complement them and complete this chapter.

Opposite: **The famous Yellow Emperor, Huang Di, is credited in one story with the discovery of fire, which he made by rubbing sticks together. He then showed his people how to use fire to cook and thus saved them from being poisoned by raw food.**

Left: **This green-glazed pottery watchtower dates from the Han dynasty. Such grave goods were used as symbolic offerings for the afterlife. The Han period is the time when the mythical heroes were incorporated into Chinese religion and beliefs.**

51

The Yellow Emperor

In traditional Chinese histories, Huang Di was revered as the greatest of the sovereigns said to have ruled China in the third millennium BCE, during its legendary ancient past. Hailed as the Yellow Emperor and ancestor of the entire Chinese race, he was also the most significant of all the culture heroes.

According to tradition, Huang Di created the wheel, boats and oars, and taught people to build roads and cut passes through forbidding mountain ranges. He invented handwriting and introduced the arts of pottery and music to China, although in some accounts Fu Xi, Nü Wa or Di Ku was credited with developing the first musical instruments (see page 41). He also devised the first calendar, and gave people instruments with which to measure the movements of the stars and planets.

Huang Di also taught the selective breeding of animals and the seasonal planting of crops and trees – so building on the legacy of his predecessor and rival Shen Nong, who had introduced agriculture to China (see page 46). Huang Di was said to have driven away the wild animals that preyed on humans, although this was also credited to Nü Wa.

One of Huang Di's gifts to the Chinese people was boats. This carved coral model shows a typical fishing vessel, with one fisherman hauling his full net from the sea and another putting some of the catch into a wicker basket.

Victory over Chaos

The Yellow Emperor made the first armor, and in the earliest surviving myths he was a warrior deity who triumphed in a series of conflicts. He fought the Fiery Emperor Yan Di, a god of war Chi You, the single-legged deity Kui and others. It was emphasized that Huang Di did not go to war out of a love of violence, but in order to restore order when it was challenged. Around him grew up a mythology depicting him as a great general who won prolonged and heroic battles against his half-brother Yan Di and other foes (see pages 56–61).

After defeating Yan Di, Huang Di became chief of the gods, assuming overall authority as God of the Center. His defeated rival became God of the South; his great ancestor Fu Xi was God of the East. Huang Di then sent Shao Hao to be God of the West and Zhuan Xu to be God of the North. Huang Di had four faces, one facing each of the cardinal points. He could not be outwitted or defeated because he could see in all directions at once. In one myth, preserved in the third-century CE text *The Myriad Sayings of Master Jiang*, the four emperors of the cardinal directions rose up against him, but he defeated them without trouble.

Immortal Secrets

The Yellow Emperor was also said to have been the first ruler to establish and organize religious ceremony in China. According to some accounts,

Mythical Emperors

The early historians gave China's nine mythical emperors dates of reign, an order of succession, and real names and titles (listed first and second respectively, and translated where possible). The dates, were, of course, also mythical, and since most of the rulers were originally gods, their activity tended to move between Earth and Heaven. The first three are often called the Three Sovereigns or Three Emperors, the last three are the Sage Kings, of whom Confucius had a high opinion.

c. 2900 BCE **Fu Xi, Tai Hao (Great Brilliance)**
Divine being with a serpent's body. Brother and/or husband of Nü Wa who discovered the oracular diagrams. Taught people to cook and fish with nets.

c. 2800 BCE **Shen Nong, Yan Di (Fiery Emperor)**
Divine being with a bird's head and a human body. He invented the cart and the plow, and taught people to clear land to grow crops. Tried out medicinal plants on himself.

c. 2700 BCE **Xian Yuan, Huang Di (Yellow Emperor)**
Wise ruler and great warrior who invented wooden houses, boats, bows and arrows and writing. According to Daoists he dreamed of a land where people lived in harmony with nature. Regarded as ancestor of the Chinese people.

c. 2600 BCE **Jin Tian, Shao Hao (Lesser Brilliance)**
Son of a weaver goddess and the planet Venus whom she met while rafting on the Milky Way. Shao Hao introduced the twenty-five-string lute.

c. 2500 BCE **Gao Yang, Zhuan Xu**
Grandson of Huang Di, nephew of Shao Hao. Harsh ruler who ordered the link between Heaven and Earth to be destroyed. Established male supremacy.

c. 2400 BCE **Gao Xin, Di Ku**
Cousin of Zhuan Xu. Encouraged musical composition and ordered the musician You Chui to develop many new instruments.

c. 2300 BCE **Yao, Tang Di Yao**
Model emperor praised by Confucius who lived frugally and cared for the people. His ministers were wise and able but not his son, so he chose his son-in-law Shun as his successor.

c. 2300 BCE **Shun, Yu Di Shun**
Praised as "sage emperor" by Confucius. Protected from hardships by Heaven, which sent birds to weed his crops and animals to pull his plow. Standardized weights and measures, regulated rivers and divided China into twelve provinces.

c. 2200 BCE **Yu, Da Yu (Yu the Great)**
Founder of the Xia dynasty. Son of Gun who was appointed to control the floods. Completed the work begun by his father, with the aid of dragons.

Huang Di, or Xian Yuan, was given a pill that granted immortality by Tai Yi Huang Ren, the spirit of a mountain in Sichuan Province. Huang Di visited the peak with Chi Jiang Ziyou, who stayed on to serve the mountain god, surviving on the flowers that grew on the gently sloping sides of the peak and gradually losing his Earthly body in favor of a heavenly one. This Chi Jiang Ziyou later became the divine archer Yi and performed many heroic feats. Xian Yuan was the name of an early deity of uncertain attributes who was linked to the Yellow Emperor; in a similar way, Fu Xi was sometimes named Tai Hao and the identities of Shen Nong and Yan Di mingled – probably as real names and titles. The alternative names had enduring appeal: in his Tang-era work *Seven Tomes from the Cloudy Shelf* (see page 51) Wang Chuan called the Yellow Emperor Xian Yuan. (Legends about Di Ku, Di Jun and Shun also have so many similarities that it is likely they were three names for the same figure, perhaps drawn from the conflicting versions of three different peoples inhabiting China in prehistory.)

Huang Di revealed the key to eternal life in a book about medicine; he also knew how to make gold, for the tablet of immortality brought with it the secrets of alchemy. With Fu Xi and Shen Nong, he was sometimes viewed as a god of healing and medicine. His young empress Lei Zu was traditionally credited with being the first human to breed worms for silk; in some accounts she was given silk and instructed in the method by the goddess Lady Silkworm (see pages 62–63).

A 6th-century terracotta figure playing the lute or qin, an instrument thousands of years old. In the 3rd-century BCE text, *Annals of Master Lu*, Di Ku commanded a divine craftsman to make the first musical instruments. Di Ku then showed people how to play music so wonderful that the pheasants and phoenixes danced and capered with delight.

53

Huang Di's Black Bead

One tale about the Yellow Emperor recounts how, as he travelled between Earth and Heaven, he lost one of his most precious possessions and had to turn to lesser deities for help.

High in the forbidding Kunlun Mountains stood Huang Di's wondrous city, with the propitious number of nine gates and nine water wells on each side. The city was dominated by an exquisitely wrought palace, surrounded by walkways and balconies of white jade that seemed to give off an otherworldly glimmer in the dark. From its main gate, which opened to the east, the sun's first appearance could be seen each morning. Hu Wu, a tiger deity with a human face, nine tails and sharp claws, guarded the Kunlun palace for the Yellow Emperor.

All around the palace clustered marvellous trees, which never dropped their leaves and bore precious crops of pearls, jasper and jade as well as succulent pears. A rice paddy lay nearby, but when he was in residence Huang Di preferred to eat the white cream said to ooze from the jade found on nearby Mishan Hill. He was so enamored of this food that he took some of the precious stone and buried it on Zhongshan Mountain, where it multiplied; and from that time all the gods in the celestial realm chose to eat the jade mined on Zhongshan peak.

It gave Huang Di great pleasure to visit his Kunlun residence and he stayed there as often as he could. He loved to view the palace from his hanging garden on nearby Huaijiang Mountain. A gaggle of beautiful red phoenixes was constantly seen about the place, for they had been instructed by Huang Di to care for the building and maintain its majestic appearance.

The Search for Imperial Treasure

One day as he travelled back to the heavenly realm after a stay at the palace, Huang Di dropped his favorite black bead, a jewel he prized above all others, on the banks of the River Chishui. The Yellow Emperor was greatly distressed and looked around wildly for the bead, but he could not find it. Back in Heaven he called a host of lesser gods to his aid. First he sent Zhi ("Knowledge"), one of

Beijing black glass beads adorn this so-called Mandarin chain. Beads were an important symbol of rank in China and their size, color and arrangement denoted status. Mandarin chains were worn by the emperor and the nobility during the Qing dynasty, their inspiration coming from Tibetan rosaries from which they copied exactly the same number of beads: 108.

the most intelligent of the gods, to search for it. Zhi walked all the paths near Chishui and trampled the fields and undergrowth – but he could not find the treasure. He returned sadly to Huang Di, and delivered the bad news. The Yellow Emperor was not downhearted, however, and dispatched three-headed Li Zhu, confident that his six shining eyes would find the lost jewel. But he too failed to recover it.

Then Huang Di sent Chi Gou ("Complex Debate"), but although this god was skilled in argument and could dazzle with the slickness and eloquence of his speech, he could not find the bead. Huang Di was growing desperate now and as a last resort sent Xiang Wang ("Formless") on the mission. The Yellow Emperor did not hold out much hope because Xiang Wang always seemed to lack direction and to follow his impulses.

Xiang Wang arrived at the River Chishui and sauntered along looking idly about. At once he spied the bead lying in the undergrowth. He picked it up and wandered back to Heaven with the prize. Huang Di was delighted to have the bead back, but also more than a little puzzled that such a careless fellow should have managed to find it. He pondered on this paradox, and came to the conclusion that Xiang Wang's instinctive abilities were as effective as those of more disciplined and skilled deities. Huang Di honored Xiang Wang by giving him the bead to look after.

Responsibility did not change Xiang Wang's character, however, and without much thought he slipped the bead into his sleeve and went about his usual business. One day a lithe goddess with a lively sense of mischief heard that Xiang Wang was caring for the bead and determined to relieve him of it as a prank. She found it easy to distract him and took the imperial treasure away. But when Huang Di heard that she had stolen his jewel, he flew into a rage and sent several gods after her. Overcome with fear, the young woman threw the bead into her mouth and swallowed it. Then she leaped into the Wenchuan River. The instant she hit the water she was transformed, her soft skin taking on a dragon's scales and her delicate face becoming that of a snorting horse. She took the name Qi Xiang, and became the goddess of the river.

This version of the myth of the black bead is told by a fourth-century-BCE Daoist scholar who sought to recast the myth – essentially, to reinvent it – in terms of his own philosophy. Specifically, he aimed to prove the superiority of primitive and instinctual nature (exemplified by "Formless") over knowledge, language skills or even natural abilities such as good eyesight.

The rivers of China, great and small, each had their own deity. According to an alternative version of the black bead myth, when the recovered bead was subsequently stolen by a mischievous goddess, it was Huang Di's helper Xiang Wang ("Formless") who leaped into the waters and became transformed into a river god.

A Battle of the Elements

Strife rocked Heaven, and Huang Di and Yan Di, divine rulers who shared authority over the universe, resolved to do battle to achieve total supremacy. The Yellow Emperor, fearless in conflict, prepared to defend natural order against his half-brother.

Huang Di and Yan Di drew up their vast armies on the Zhoulu Plain, now in Hebei Province. Wild beasts swelled the ranks on both sides, while hawks and vultures darkened the skies over the battlefield. But the conflict was quickly over, for Yan Di was already an old man who lacked energy and resourcefulness while Huang Di was a virile warrior god, full of wiles and bursting with vitality. Yan Di fled to the south.

In the earliest accounts, the clash was an elemental one, for Yan Di (Blazing Ruler or Fiery Emperor) was armed with fire while the Yellow Emperor fought with water, and water inevitably won. After his victory, Huang Di established order throughout the universe, taking up position as God of the Center, assisted by four gods of the cardinal directions (see page 52). But he had to face many challenges to his authority.

When Gu, a fierce dragon god with a human face, teamed up with another deity named Qin Pi to kill the god Bao Jiang, Huang Di acted swiftly. Gu and Qin Pi were summarily dispatched by Huang Di's executioners. But upon his death Qin Pi was transformed into a monstrous osprey with tiger's feet, who ever afterward brought strife and bloodshed wherever he went. Gu meanwhile

became a hideous yellow-spotted owl with blood-red talons, bringer of drought and famine.

On another occasion, a minor god named Wei dared to kill Jia Yu, a divine serpent with a man's face, but Huang Di was quick to punish the upstart. Wei was captured, dragged ignominiously to Shushu Mountain, in the west, and tied to a tree. Huang Di, who had knowledge of death and possessed the pill of immortality, brought Jia Yu to the Kunlun Mountains and restored him to life. Unfortunately, Jia Yu was transformed into a fierce beast who preyed on humans until the divine archer Yi dispatched him.

Glorious Victory Procession

After his resounding defeat of Yan Di, Huang Di drove in a victory procession to make sacrifices on the holiest of all mountains, Taishan. His ivory chariot was pulled by a team of sure-footed elephants and guarded by six flying dragons on each side, while red phoenixes capered in the sky overhead. Winged snakes also attended. Tigers and wolves went ahead of the vehicle, together with the wind god Feng Bo and the master of rains Yu Shi who cleaned the dusty mountain road as the emperor approached.

At the very head of the procession was the strongman Chi You, who had been a follower of Yan Di but now had to answer to Huang Di. This tall, broad-chested god of war was one of eighty-two brothers from the south. These fearsome giants had unbreakable heads of bronze, with sharp horns and foreheads of iron. The hair on their metal scalps stood up straight and sharp like the blades of knives and they each had four eyes. Their feet were hooved like those of a strong ox. Their teeth were unbreakable, too, for their diet consisted of iron, sand and pebbles.

Chi You was as obstinate as the ox he resembled and he did not take kindly to being forced into Huang Di's procession. The Yellow Emperor

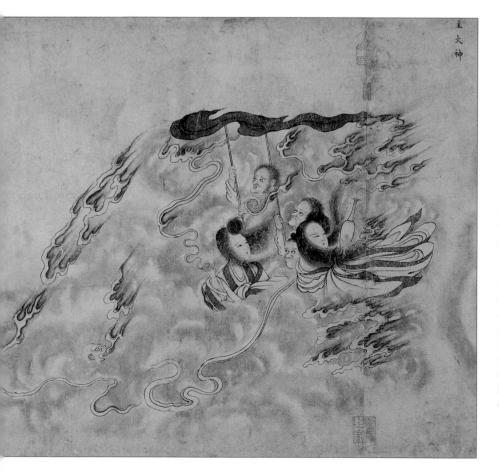

An 11th-century painted handscroll depicting the cataclysmic conflict between the forces of Huang Di and Chi You and their use of fire (*right*) and wind (*left*) respectively. Huang Di's army came under attack from the wind god Feng Bo, fighting for Chi You alongside the rain god Yu Shi, and the storm drove them back. This forced Huang Di to make use of unconventional military strategies and he sent his daughter Ba, bringer of droughts, to scorch the enemy into submission. The ruse worked, although it had detrimental results for Ba herself who was forced to live on Earth thereafter.

himself, meanwhile, was aware of Chi You's resentment and so he ordered Feng Bo and Yu Shi to watch over him. These deities often talked with the war god and in time he won them over, persuading them to help him escape. Then, rejoicing in his freedom, he returned to the south, where he tried to rouse Yan Di to further revolt – without success, for Yan Di was old and tired of conflict. Chi You's eighty-one brothers, however, were always spoiling for battle and he was also able to win the support of the Miao people, who felt that Huang Di had mistreated them. At the head of a clamoring army, which was boosted by a force of monsters and demons who also hated Huang Di, the god of war marched northward, declaring his undying hatred for the Yellow Emperor.

Huang Di was saved in battle by Feng Hou's compass-like device. This mariner's instrument dates from the 19th century, but basic lodestones were used from the 11th century.

Failed Peace Talks

Huang Di heard of Chi You's approach and set out to try to reason with him, for the Yellow Emperor was renowned as a peacemaker and was skilled in arbitration. But the talking failed to deflect Chi You from his violent purpose, and the two armies drew up on Zhoulu Plain, which was still littered with the bones of warriors who had fallen in the conflict between Huang Di and Yan Di. In the Yellow Emperor's ranks were slavering wolves, tigers, swift foxes, jackals and bears with claws sharp enough to shred a man's skin. He also had the dragon Ying Long and his daughter Ba ("Drought") as well as several other deities on his side.

But for all his strength, Huang Di was bested in the first exchanges, particularly after Chi You used magic to envelop the battlefield in thick fog. The animals and monsters in Huang Di's army circled helplessly, thrown into a panic by the thick white blanket. Chi You and his fearless warriors moved purposefully about, stealthily bringing death to their enemies.

Huang Di ordered several charges to try and break free of the fog, but everywhere his men went the mist seemed to follow and they soon lost their bearings entirely. Then the Yellow Emperor was saved by an ingenious old man named Feng Hou. Huang Di saw this man with his head bowed deep in thought and rounded on him, assuming he was sleeping. But Feng Hou was close to a solution to their problems. Despite the roar of battle and the clamor of the frightened animals, he concentrated his mind in creative thought and invented a device like a compass that could show each of the cardinal directions. He set it in the front of Huang Di's chariot in the form of a statue of a fairy whose arm forever pointed to the south. With the help of this wonderful instrument, the emperor and his army burst out of the encircling gloom.

Huang Di now turned to his divine ally and subordinate, Ying Long, who had the power to unleash devastating rainstorms. He ordered the dragon to attack Chi You's army with water, but before Ying Long could act, the wind god Feng Bo and the master of rains Yu Shi – who were fighting on Chi You's side – let loose a devastating storm and Huang Di's vast army was driven back. Pondering yet another defeat, Huang Di thought of his daughter Ba who had the power of scorching heat at her disposal, and asked her to launch an attack. It was devastatingly effective, but it was the undoing of Ba herself, for she lost the power to climb to Heaven and was forced to dwell on Earth. Ba was an unwelcome guest, disliked as a bringer of drought and insulted wherever she went.

58

Mythical Beasts

Jia Yu's transformation into a terrifying beast, with a tiger's flesh-ripping claws and a dragon's fiery breath, is just one of many examples of the strange animal hybrids that feature in Chinese myths.

Many were peaceable creatures. The qilin was one whose appearance is invariably a propitious omen. The name itself combined the characters for male and female, making the animal a living embodiment of the complementary junction of yin and yang.

As the legends would have it, individual qilin (often the head of a unicorn with other animals' parts: a horse's hooves or an ox's tail, for example) have cropped up throughout Chinese history, always to indicate the presence of some great man. One was found in the garden of Huang Di, the Yellow Emperor, and a pair were seen in the time of the great Emperor Yao. Two were spotted in Confucius's lifetime, one just before he was born, the other presaging his death when it was knocked down by a charioteer. So when, in 1414 CE, the Sultan of Malindi in East Africa sent a giraffe – the first ever to be seen in China – to the imperial court as a gift, it seemed only natural to present it to the reigning emperor, Yong Le, as a fine example of a qilin.

During Huang Di's procession to Taishan, after his victory against Yan Di, a host of immortal spirits followed his chariot, taking many remarkable forms – some with the heads of horses or birds, others with the bodies of dragons and serpents.

A strange enamelled mythical beast from the Ming dynasty that appears to be part dragon and part feline.

Divine Strategy

Chi You suffered heavy defeats following the intervention of Ba, but soon afterward the rebel forces were strengthened once again by the arrival of some members of the Kua Fu, a tribe of giants from the far north, who had been persuaded to support Chi You. The tide of the war seemed to be turning once more, and Huang Di was at a loss what to do. He put General Li Mu in charge of the imperial troops and travelled alone to the sacred peak of Taishan, where he took to his bed. But new hope came to him there in the form of a visit from a divine fairy named Xuan Nü who offered to teach him military strategy. He was delighted to accept, and over the following days learned many battlefield maneuvers. Then he mined a magic copper from the Kunlun Mountains with which to make new swords.

Huang Di's troops, equipped with these peerless weapons and directed by the emperor with his newly acquired military expertise, soon brought Chi You's warriors to the brink of defeat. The imperial army trapped the rebels in the center of the plain and surrounded them. The flying dragon Ying Long was a terrible sight, sweeping down from above to exact revenge, killing several of the Kua Fu giants.

Swift Justice

Finally Chi You was captured and brought in chains before the emperor – and Huang Di ordered the rebel's immediate execution. Even in victory, however, Huang Di's followers were terrified of Chi You's awesome strength and they kept him chained and handcuffed until after he had been put to death. Ying Long himself performed the execution. Then the chains and handcuffs, drenched in the blood of a god of war, were hurled out onto the plain, far from any dwelling. As they landed they were transformed into a grove of maple trees, whose reddish leaves are whipped against each other by the wind and seem eternally to complain of the war god's cruel death.

After the battle, Ying Long, like Huang Di's goddess daughter Ba, found that he had lost an essential element of his divinity and could no longer climb to Heaven. Despite his great contribution to Huang Di's victory, the dragon was cursed to live forever on Earth. He travelled sadly to the far south where he still roams among the peaks and mountain lakes.

Chi You was renowned as the first to mine metal and to introduce metal weapons to humankind. In some accounts, he was linked with a deity who tried to race against the sun but died of thirst and exhaustion; the connection characterizes Chi You as an overreacher, whose false pride made punishment and death inevitable. He was sometimes seen as a primal rebel, the first to flout authority – but later mythological treatments viewed him with sympathy. It is characteristic of the Chinese tradition that rulers or deities who rise up but are defeated – such as Chi You or Yan Di – are viewed in the myths with respect and sympathy, despite their failure.

Zhou-period bronze swords, tinged green with age, closely resemble the image conveyed of Huang Di's Kunlun copper swords. It was said that the ore was fire-red but when cast as a weapon it turned green and transparent like a fragile jewel. It was tough enough to slice through jade, and it gave off an eery white light as if cold death itself were seeping out from the blade, searching for its victims.

Huang Di and Xing Tian

After defeating Chi You, Huang Di was faced with yet another challenge to his authority. A vast giant named Xing Tian arose in the south, determined to do away with the Yellow Emperor, and the two fought a titanic struggle that began in Heaven and ended on Changyang Mountain.

As he marched north, Xing Tian shook with fury, for he was a long-time enemy of Huang Di. He had once been a minister of Yan Di, and when the old god was defeated (see page 56) Xing Tian fled south with him. He had wanted to join the revolt led by Chi You, but Yan Di would not allow it. But when Chi You was vanquished, too, Xing Tian set off to confront Huang Di – then in residence in Heaven.

The giant shrugged off the challenge of one guard after another until he came face-to-face with the Yellow Emperor himself. Xing Tian contemptuously challenged Huang Di to fight – and the emperor rose at once and seized his best sword. A mighty conflict ensued, in which the two warriors tested their strength to the utmost and the air around them shook with their cries.

Without noticing, they left Heaven behind and fought their way across the slopes of Changyang Mountain in western China. Here Huang Di saw his opportunity and with a single stroke sliced off the giant's head. From the top of his vast body it crashed to the ground, making the mountains themselves shudder. But Xing Tian did not fall, for the blow had not killed him: headless, he could not see but still had strength for the fight.

The giant lowered himself onto his haunches and groped around on the slopes for his head. As his huge fists smote here and there, they smashed whole cliffs and entire forests. Huang Di meanwhile had the advantage. He saw where the head had landed and quickly cut open the adjoining mountain so that it rolled into the crevice. Then he sealed the mountain once more and the giant's head was encased in rock.

Lady Silkworm

Huang Di marked his victories over Chi You and Xing Tian with a celebration in his palace. While songs of triumph rang out, the exhausted emperor rested on his throne, secure in the knowledge that he had restored order to the world.

Then, in the midst of this merry-making, came a strange apparition: Can Nü ("Lady Silkworm"), the goddess of silkworms, appeared wrapped from head to toe in horsehide. She bowed to Huang Di and offered him two delicately colored reels of the finest silk, one golden and the other silver.

There were various accounts of the life of the silkworm goddess and of how she first made silk. In one the goddess was a star deity named Jian Si; in another she was identified with Huang Di's empress, Lei Zu (some sources say Xiling Ji). But in the most complete account, she was the beautiful and faithful daughter of a mortal man.

According to this tale, Can Nü's father left home and travelled far away; for an entire year his daughter pined for him and cared for the home. One day as she groomed the family horse, she murmured that she would willingly marry anyone who could find her father and bring him home. In that instant the horse bolted and Can Nü could only watch in despair as it galloped away.

Within a few days the resourceful stallion had tracked down the young woman's father. He was living at his ease in a distant place, without a thought for his daughter's needs. The stallion approached him and by stamping its feet and waving its head indicated that it wanted to return home at once. The father, wondering if his daughter was in trouble, leaped onto the horse's back.

The young woman danced with delight when she saw her father returning. They embraced tenderly and she told him how much she had missed him and how the horse, perhaps sensing this, had

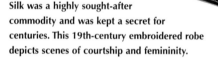

Silk was a highly sought-after commodity and was kept a secret for centuries. This 19th-century embroidered robe depicts scenes of courtship and femininity.

left one day to bring him home. From that day on, the father lavished care upon the horse, providing regular grooming and extra hay. But the creature was distressed and whenever it saw Can Nü it stamped its feet and and neighed as if in pain.

After some time the father asked his daughter if she could explain the horse's behavior and she told him of the promise she had made – to marry anyone who brought her father home. The father ordered that the affair be kept a secret, and then he shot the horse with an arrow.

Now he thought his troubles were over. He skinned the animal and laid its hide out to dry. Then he had to go away again. That day his daughter and a friend were talking in the yard and Can Nü kicked the animal skin and laughed at it.

But as she turned away, still laughing, the skin rose up like a ghost, wrapped itself around her and whipped her away into the countryside.

Terrified, the friend ran after them but she could do nothing. When the father returned and learned what had happened, he searched far and wide for several days. Eventually, he found Can Nü, still wrapped in the skin, hanging in an unfa-miliar tree. The poor man cried out: she was no longer his fair daughter, for she had been changed into a worm. As she wriggled she moved her head like a horse, and a fine thread spewed from her mouth.

Can Nü's friend named the tree "mulberry," a word derived from "mourning" (*sang*). People experimented with the thread and found they could use it to make fine cloths; they took tree cuttings and planted them, and, in time, learned how to breed silkworms for the thread.

The Fruit of the Worm

Chinese sericulture – breeding worms and producing silk – is so ancient that its origins are swathed in myth, but by the middle of the third millennium BCE it had already been discovered that the silkworm's cocoon could be unravelled and woven into a soft cloth.

All that was needed to do this were the worms and the mulberry trees on which they fed – each day eating several times their own weight in leaves. Sericulture became a thriving cottage industry in rural China, with one of its bases in Henan Province in the north of the country.

For hundreds of years, the methods used were kept completely secret. Silk was not exported from China until the first millennium BCE. Later, under the Han dynasty (206 BCE–220 CE), a major trade in silk with Europe became established.

The cloth travelled along the Silk Road – a caravan trail, which ran almost 13,000 kilometers from Shanghai on the China Sea to Cadiz in southwestern Spain through Ankara and Byzantium (Istanbul), across the Adriatic to Italy and then along the Mediterranean coast. Han rulers made diplomatic presents of silk garments and used the luxurious cloth to pacify raiders.

Tussah silk, a less fine cloth that is made using wild rather than domesticated silkworms, was produced in India from c.1400 BCE. But the secret of how Chinese silk was made was kept until the mid-sixth century CE, when two Persian monks smuggled silkworms and mulberry seeds in bamboo canes to Byzantium at the request of the emperor, Justinian I, and sericulture was subsequently established in Europe. It had spread to Japan in the third century CE when, according to traditional accounts, a group of concubines secretly exported the Chinese method.

The Cowherd and the Girl Weaver

The stars in the glittering night sky inspired many Chinese myths, including that of the graceful Girl Weaver, a goddess of luminous beauty who caught the eye of a resourceful peasant. The tale accounts for the existence of the Milky Way in the heavens.

In the time when the worlds of gods and men were far closer than they are now, a strong, handsome cowherd fell in love with the Girl Weaver. She had woven the clouds that adorn the heavens, covering the nakedness of the blue skies day and night, and was the granddaughter of Xi Wang Mu, Queen Mother of the West.

Then, the Milky Way was a sparkling terrestrial river whose clear, shallow waters flowed over multi-colored pebbles and stones. On one side was

the abode of the gods and goddesses; on the other, the land of mortal men and women. The cowherd settled on the banks of the river, where he was able to grow enough food to survive. But he was unhappy, since he longed for company.

The cowherd's only companion was a loyal ox. Upset by his master's loneliness, the ox one day spoke aloud in a human voice and told him of the beautiful Girl Weaver who loved to bathe in the river. The next day the cowherd concealed

A Kingdom of Birds

The mythology of the Girl Weaver influenced accounts of the god Shao Hao's birth. His mother was a divine weaver who fell in love while taking her pleasure on the celestial river of the Milky Way.

Shao Hao's mother, a beautiful fairy named Huange, worked on the heavenly looms. She loved to launch a raft on the gentle current of the Milky Way and paddle upstream to visit the glorious mulberry tree named Qiongsang that stood near the Western Sea. Beneath the tree's branches a good-looking young man would wait for her; he was the morning star.

Sometimes they took to the river together and he would sing and play a zither as the waters lapped against the fragile raft and the moon kept silent witness in the sky above. From

precious jade they made a model of a dove and set it on the raft's mast, where it swung about to indicate the direction of the wind – this later inspired people to make weathercocks. They made the mast out of cassia and hung sweet-smelling grasses from it, so that delightful fragrances played over them as they rested against each other. They became lovers and in due course Shao Hao was born.

He grew into a handsome youth, and was so capable that his great uncle Huang Di named him God of the Western Heavens. In his prime, Shao Hao

himself on the bank and watched as the goddess and her six sisters undressed and plunged into the stream. The clear waters grew opaque and hid their nakedness. The cowherd took his chance, leaped out and seized the Girl Weaver's clothes, agreeing to return them only if she agreed to marry him. She acquiesced, for in any case she felt a thrill of desire for this peasant on the bank.

The fruit of their marriage was a boy and a girl. But when the Girl Weaver's grandmother discovered that she had married a mortal, she was incensed and her messengers came to take her away. Carrying the children, her husband ran after her, thinking he could ford the shallow Milky Way and pursue her. When the cowherd came to where the river should have been, he found things changed beyond recognition. He looked about for the stream's familiar sparkling flow; then, rolling his eyes upward, saw it running across the heavens. Xi Wang Mu had lifted the river from the Earth and set it in the night sky. Distraught, he returned home. That night his old ox told him that it was about to die, but that its hide had magic qualities that would enable the cowherd to climb to Heaven. When the beast passed away, the cowherd sorrowfully skinned it and, with the hide, resumed his pursuit.

In Heaven he reached the bank of the Milky Way and could see the Girl Weaver on the far side, but Xi Wang Mu spotted him and transformed the river into a raging torrent. He toiled for days to empty it with a ladle, and this show of devotion led Xi Wang Mu to announce that on one night each year – the seventh day of the seventh month – a flock of magpies would form a bridge across the Milky Way, permitting the two lovers to meet.

travelled to the five mountains of the Eastern Paradise and established a kingdom populated entirely by birds. As its ruler he took the form of a vulture and oversaw a vast feathered bureaucracy, with the phoenix as his Lord Chancellor. He put the hawk in charge of the law, and to the pigeon he gave responsibility for education, while the changing weather across the four seasons he placed in the charge of the pheasant, the quail, the shrike and the swallow. For many years he ruled the bird kingdom with wisdom, but eventually he went back to the west, leaving his son Chong in charge of the birds. With another of his sons, Ru Shou, he settled on Changliu Mountain and ruled over the Western Heavens. Father and son together were responsible for the sunset.

65

Tales of Everyday People

Chinese mythology has a rich popular tradition that complements the body of stories preserved by ancient philosophers and scholars. The tales told by the peasants document life in the country and the origins of foods and animals useful from day to day rather than the distant and heroic exploits of gods and goddesses.

The Five Grains and the skills of plowing and planting were introduced to China by the god of agriculture Shen Nong (see page 46). But there were many popular tales of the origins of particular plants, including that of rice. According to one version, people had the dog to thank for the discovery of this staple food. Before Yu had conquered the destructive floods (see pages 88–89), people faced starvation. They had to abandon farming and survive as best they could by hunting. Then in one waterlogged corner of China, a peasant saw a dog running from a wet, marshy field with yellowing grasses dangling from its tail. When he caught the animal and examined it more closely he found seeds in the ears of the grasses; he collected as many as he could and with his fellow villagers planted them in the fields. The crop that resulted was rice, and ever afterward people had a special regard for dogs, particularly at the time of the rice harvest. Food was traditionally put out for dogs at the first meal after the crop was brought in.

The cultivation of the Five Grains, introduced by the Lord of Earth and divine farmer Shen Nong, enabled Chinese civilization to flourish. This 14th-century piece, attributed to Zheng Ji, depicts the threshing, winnowing and sorting of rice.

A Wife's Undying Devotion

The story of the loyal wife Meng Jiang is one of the oldest surviving folk tales in China, predating the building of the Great Wall. Two ancient families, the Meng and the Jiang, lived on adjacent pieces of land, separated by a wall. Both families planted a climbing pumpkin plant on their side of the wall, and when they reached the top the two entwined and united, producing a vast fruit. They agreed to cut it down and split it, but inside they discovered a beautiful baby girl. They named her Meng Jiang, from their surnames, and shared her upbringing.

These ivory pumpkin boxes date from the 19th century and contain carved figures. When the Meng and Jiang families cut down a pumpkin they found inside it a baby girl whom they named Meng Jiang.

Meng Jiang grew up in a land that was riven by fear: no one was safe from the emperor's henchmen, who would arrive unannounced and haul people away. The emperor was encountering problems with his ambitious scheme to build the Great Wall, and a wise man had told him that he must bury 10,000 living men to make the wall stand tall and firm. Then one day another wise man said that the same effect could be achieved by killing and burying one man named Wan ("Ten Thousand"). The emperor was pleased with the new advice and sent out messengers to find Wan.

However, this unfortunate individual heard of the plan and took refuge in Meng Jiang's garden. That very night the beautiful maiden came out to bathe. She lay naked in the cool waters, murmuring that if any man saw her now she would marry him. Wang's voice rang out, informing her that he had seen her. She kept her promise and married him, but the emperor's soldiers interrupted the wedding and took Wan away.

Meng Jiang was distraught, and she vowed to honor her husband's memory. She travelled to the Great Wall, hoping somehow to find his mortal remains. But when she saw the endless extent of the fortifications she slumped to the ground in despair. At that moment the wall collapsed directly behind her, miraculously revealing the bones of the dead man.

The story of Meng Jiang's loyalty was told far and wide – and even the emperor came to hear of it. He summoned her to appear before him and the moment she entered the imperial court he was captivated by her beauty and resolved to wed her. No woman was permitted to refuse an offer of marriage from the emperor, but Meng Jiang did place certain conditions on her acceptance. She asked for a funeral feast for her husband lasting forty-nine days; requested an altar forty-nine feet tall to be placed by the river where she could honor him; and begged the emperor and all his courtiers to attend the commemoration.

The emperor agreed to all her requests. At the ceremony he and his courtiers watched curiously as Meng Jiang clambered to the top of the funerary altar but then gasped with horror as she launched a stinging attack on the emperor's heartlessness. Then she flung herself to her death into the river, leaving them crying out in disbelief.

The emperor, who throughout the proceedings had kept his anger on a tight rein, now unleashed it. He ordered his men to chop up her body and smash her bones. But they could not catch this delicate and devoted woman, for her corpse turned into a shoal of tiny silver fish that swam away, fleet as light, in the deep stream.

67

Divine Animals

A lot of popular myths feature the wild and farm animals encountered daily by peasants. Some beasts have semi-divine powers and others the ability to undergo shapeshifting transformations; many stories simply explain how animals came by their appearance.

Foxes played a major role in the animal myths. They were said to be masters of transformation, their most common human forms being old men, poverty-stricken scholars, or nimble-footed maidens. The fox was also believed to be able to start a fire by hitting the ground with its bushy tail.

Seeing a fox was usually a bad omen, for they were thought to be a shape taken by ghosts. But the creature was also said to have the power to see the future and bestow good fortune. The fox's most common role in popular myth, however, was as a mischief-maker (see box opposite).

The Horns of Oxen

One story describes why some oxen have twisted horns. A maiden stopped to drink from a mountain stream. Her thirst quenched, she felt hungry and picked up a leafy plant floating in the water. The leaves bore the tooth marks of some great beast

A farmer calls his ox and calf to him in this 11th-century handscroll. Oxen appear in many Chinese myths, and tradition has it that the ox was sent to Earth to help man produce food.

but she ate the main part, which was untouched. It had a sweet taste. Some weeks later she found she was pregnant, and in time she gave birth to a beautiful girl.

The young girl pestered her mother with questions about her father. The mother told the story of how she had become pregnant and confessed that on the eve of the birth she had had a dream in which a sacred ox from the mountains had revealed himself as the father. At once the girl determined to go and seek him out. The mother suggested the daughter take the sweet-tasting leafy plant with her and offer it to the mountain oxen until she found one that ate the leaves and not the flesh – then she would have found her father.

The Friendly Fox

A wily fox played a good-natured trick on a farmer who had a fondness for wine. In the farmyard stood a vast pile of straw, part of which had been hollowed out as the stalks were taken and used.

The mischievous beast made its den in the hole and often stopped to talk to the farmer. In order to converse with a human it took the form of a whiskery old man. The farmer knew its true identity, but it did not bother him.

One evening the old man invited the farmer inside the stack of straw, where to his astonishment he found a row of splendidly decorated rooms. The friendly old man served his guest with fragrant tea and a glass or two of exceptional wine.

Over the following weeks the farmer often observed the old man creeping away at dusk and then returning at dawn. Curious, he asked where the trips took him and the old fellow confessed that he went away to taste wines with a friend. Having enjoyed his visit to the straw stack, the farmer asked to go with the old man, who at first refused, but finally agreed. The two set off at once, carried up magically into the night air as if driven before a strong wind.

They landed in a city and went to a restaurant crowded with men drinking and singing riotously. The old man seated the farmer on a raised gallery and went invisibly among the diners below, bringing back fine wines and foods for his guest. When a waiter appeared with dessert, the farmer asked the fox if he could taste some. The animal replied that he could not approach the waiter, as he was an upright man. The farmer was stricken, realizing his own loss of virtue since he had begun to consort with the animal; and he promised himself that he would improve.

Perhaps the realization brought him to his senses, for in that instant he had the sensation of falling. He awoke on the floor of the restaurant, surrounded by the diners; instead of the gallery, he saw that he had been sitting on a roof beam. People were enthralled when he told his story and as a sign of appreciation they funded his return journey, for it turned out that the restaurant was a very long way from his home.

The girl climbed into the most forbidding reaches of the mountain range – and eventually she found such an ox. She tracked it to a cave where it lived with a herd of oxen. Then she settled nearby in the hollow trunk of a dead tree.

After several days, the ox recognized the human girl as his daughter and revealed his identity to her. She danced with happiness, and for many months the girl remained in her makeshift dwelling – but the brutal cold of winter was approaching. The ox tried to persuade her to go back to the village lower down the mountain, but she refused – so he resolved to build her a proper shelter. He used the horns of his fellow oxen; the animals twisted the horns as they removed them from their heads. The father erected a splendid house for his faithful child. As he declared that he had finished, some oxen stopped halfway through twisting their horns – and they are the ancestors of cattle with twisted horns.

THE SAGE KINGS

Yao, Shun and Yu the Great, China's three Sage Kings, exist on the cusp between mythology and history. Although they move in a world of dragons and gods, they themselves are recognizably human, and the achievements credited to them are mostly ones accomplished at some time or another by genuine, flesh-and-blood rulers. However embroidered their legends may have become, it is at least conceivable that real monarchs of those names did rule regions of China at some time in prehistory.

The trio owe much of their fame to Confucius. Although they rate only a handful of mentions in the Analects, the references are always eulogistic. The three were, simply, the first and most venerable of the ancients to whom the great political philosopher looked back for examples of correct monarchical deportment and good government. As such, they set a model for future generations. The highest praise that Confucius could find for any subsequent ruler of China was to say that, "Even Yao or Shun could not have found cause to criticize him."

Confucius himself evidently thought of the three as real historical personalities. In so doing he was following tradition, which categorized Yao and Shun as two of the last three of the nine emperors who supposedly ruled China in pre-dynastic times (see page 53).

Yu's situation was rather different. He was chosen by Shun as his successor, just as Shun had been nominated by Yao. But Yu passed on the throne to his own son, thereby starting a tradition of hereditary monarchy that laid the framework for subsequent dynastic rule. The line he started, the Xia, is traditionally listed as the first of China's many dynasties, even though archaeologists have still to find conclusive proof that it ever existed outside of legend.

Whatever the historical reality, the mythological role of the Sage Kings in the Chinese worldview as builders of order and civilization is clear, and the tales elaborated around their names reflect that fact. In the stories, they are constantly at war with the forces of chaos, battling floods, fighting monsters and placating capricious deities. What sets them apart from others is their unwavering altruism: all their thoughts and all their heroic efforts are devoted single-mindedly to bettering the lot of the long-suffering Chinese people.

Opposite: Red was a highly auspicious color, corresponding to fire and the south. Deep red indicated imperial approval, and the dragon was the most important of all imperial symbols.

Below: An ancient bronze cooking cauldron. Yu divided China into nine provinces. Ores from each were used to make nine tripod cauldrons that were passed down from ruler to ruler and became important symbols of imperial power.

The Emperor Yao and His Courtiers

Though he could still converse with gods, Yao was the first fully human Chinese sovereign. For the people of later ages, he was also the best – the very model of a just and virtuous king. Confucius eulogized him, and declared: "Greatest, as lord and ruler, was Yao."

As the philosophers and historians told it, there never was such a monarch as the Emperor Yao. In the schematizations of early history and myth that became popular in Han times, he was the seventh of the nine mythical emperors or sovereigns, following in the footsteps of the Yellow Emperor, Shao Hao and two less celebrated successors. But while his predecessors were fairly obviously figures of legend, moving in a world of magic and enchantment, Yao and his chosen heir Shun were treated by later generations as exemplars of wise human rule – even if the borders between the divine and Earthly realms had still to be clearly delineated in their day.

No one did more to spread the cult of Yao than Confucius, who eulogized him in the *Analects*. "Greatest, as lord and ruler, was Yao," he wrote; "truly sublime was he. How splendid his achievements were, how dazzling the marks of his culture!"

Yao was the first ruler mentioned in the Five Classics' *Book of History* (see pages 16–17), and there too his praises were sung. According to its opening paragraph, he was pious, intelligent, effortlessly accomplished and thoughtful. His courtesy was sincere and his deference to other people's wishes knew no bounds. "The influence of these qualities was felt to the four quarters of the empire," the chronicle goes on. "Thus the states were harmonized and the people transformed."

The myths portray Emperor Yao as the embodiment of intelligent and humane rule. As a monarch he sought to better the lot of the ordinary Chinese people, and throughout his reign, supposedly of nearly a century, the conduct of government remained relatively benign.

A Golden Age of Equality

Yao lived, if later philosophers are to be believed, in simple times, before manners and customs became corrupted.

According to one third-century-BCE commentator, the emperor lived on a peasant's diet of coarse millet and bitter green soup, and dressed in deerskin in winter while for summer he wore rough fibers. The writer drew the egalitarian moral: "Even a lowly gamekeeper was no worse clothed and provided for than he."

Yet this golden age of primitive equality was also a time of unparalleled natural disasters. Rivers overflowed their banks and caused terrible floods. Crops failed to ripen, and much cultivated land reverted to forest and scrub. Wild animals roamed the Middle Kingdom, attacking livestock and people. "Nowhere on Earth was there order," Confucius's disciple Mencius wrote.

Emperor Yao devoted his life to trying to rectify the situation. To help him, he could call on the services of some outstandingly able subordinates. One was Gao Yao, his minister of justice, under whose jurisdiction, it was said, "Wickedness at once disappeared." Gao's emblem was the qilin or unicorn, a magical beast with the power instinctively to tell right from wrong. Whenever the judge had to adjudicate in a dispute, he had only to bring in the animal, which would touch the guilty party with its horn.

Yao's Observatories

More enigmatic was the role of two sets of three brothers, named respectively Xi and He. The Book of History records that the four younger siblings were sent to the four points of the compass, respectively to observe the summer and winter solstice and the rising and setting sun. The role of the elder pair is not specified, though collectively the six were enjoined to "calculate the disposition of the sun, moon, stars and planets, and so manifest the seasons to all men."

The obvious interpretation is that Yao set up a network of astronomical observatories charged with regulating the calendar and keeping watch on the heavens. Some commentators, however, have seen deeper forces at work. In their view, the six personages are all aspects of a single mythological figure, Xi He, who in Shang times was identified as the mother of the ten suns.

Various imposingly large statues flank the sacred way leading to the Ming tombs, one representing the Chinese unicorn, sometimes called the qilin. These horned animals were said to have appeared in China during the reign of Huang Di, and the qilin was used during Emperor Yao's rule as the emblem of justice by Minister of Justice Gao Yao because it was said that the animal had an innate ability to discern the guilty from the innocent. A light made by burning its horn gave the user the ability to see into the future by staring into a bowl of water.

73

The Time of the Ten Suns

The greatest challenge Yao had to face came when ten suns rose together in the sky.
To combat the threat posed by the scorching heat and a drought, he needed supernatural
help from the divine archer, Yi.

"Why did Yi shoot the suns?" an ancient riddle asked. "Why did the ravens shed their feathers?" Most schoolchildren knew the answer, for the tale of the heroic bowman sent from Heaven to help rid the country of a murderous drought was one of the best-known of all Chinese legends.

The story started with a portentous event that threatened to bring catastrophe on an apocalyptic scale. One day the people of the Middle Kingdom rose at sunrise, as they usually did, only to find an hour or so later that an angry red glow on the horizon portended the arrival of a second sun. Before long a third orb was mounting the sky, and then a fourth. Throughout the day new suns kept rising until no fewer than ten were spaced out equidistantly across the blazing firmament.

Down below on Earth, the heat was intense. People cowered in their huts, trying to find shelter. Crops shrivelled in the fields, and lakes and ponds dried up. Animals collapsed from exhaustion, and all activity ceased. Faced with the greatest crisis of his reign, Yao prayed to Di Jun, God of the

A glazed earthenware tile in the form of a celestial archer on horseback, dating from the Ming-dynasty period. According to another myth, in addition to the nine suns Yi also shot the Celestial Dog, one of the animals that was said to devour the moon in times of eclipse.

Eastern Heavens, for aid. The emperor knew that if anyone in the celestial sphere could help, it was he, for he presided over the distant valley where the great Fu Shan tree grew. This was a giant mulberry in whose branches the ten suns, which in those days normally took turns to light up the sky, nested during the hours of night.

The suns chose to take their rest among the boughs for inside them were mystic birds, the jun-ravens, whose pinions carried the suns on their daily journey across the sky. These birds – indeed, the suns themselves – were the offspring of Di Jun and the goddess Xi He. Each morning she would bathe one of her children in the Sweet Springs that flow in the Sun Valley before sending it off on its life-giving journey.

Now, however, for reasons that no one ever understood, all ten suns had decided to rise at once, and only divine intervention could prevent the entire world from burning up. Realizing the extreme gravity of the situation, Di Jun heard the emperor's plea and sent his most valued assistant to help undo the damage. This was Yi, the greatest bowman on Heaven or Earth.

There was nothing unearthly in the appearance of the strapping young man who strode into Yao's presence, offering his services. Yao greeted his divine assistant eagerly, then took him to a window so he could see for himself the damage that was being done.

Yi had hoped, on first learning of his mission, to be able to settle the matter peacefully, but a single glance at the scorched land was enough to convince him that desperate measures were needed. Grasping his bow, he asked to be taken to

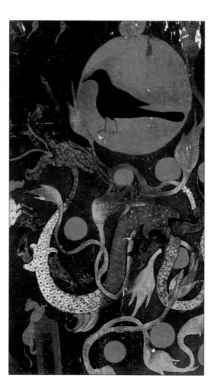

A jun-raven is depicted within a sun in this hanging silk, dating from 200 BCE, which portrays the nine suns of legend destroyed by Yao's archer, Yi.

a high tower from which he would have an unimpeded view of the heavens.

There he fitted an arrow to the string and took aim at the easternmost sun – the last of the suns to have risen. The shaft sped straight to its mark, striking the sun like a bird in flight – and, sure enough, as its light was snuffed out, a shower of black feathers fluttered down to Earth from the jun-raven within it.

Yi fired off a second arrow, then a third, and other suns fell. Word of his presence spread, and knots of anxious people began to appear on the roads and rooftops. The first cries of hope arose as the fourth and fifth suns were extinguished, and after Yi had taken aim at the sixth and seventh a roar was swelling from the now-crowded streets.

By the time he had shot down the eighth, the sky was darkened by the swirling rain of black feathers, and a glorious coolness began to spread across the land. Buoyed up by the cheers of the rescued people, Yi fitted a final arrow to his bow and sighted along its shaft at the ninth sun. As it in its turn exploded into blackness, he finally dropped the great weapon, leaving the last, westernmost sun to complete what was left of its journey to the horizon unmolested.

Yi had killed nine of the ten suns, leaving just one to illuminate the world for all future time. He had made himself a hero of humankind and had won the eternal gratitude of Emperor Yao. But time would tell that he had done so at the cost of making enemies in Heaven. He would have cause to rue the divine wrath in time to come.

The Elixir of Life

Banished from Heaven by Di Jun, Yi went in search of the magic potion that could restore his lost immortality. But the drug ended up in the wrong hands, and the hero had to undertake a fearsome quest to try to undo the damage.

When Yi had shot down the nine suns, he quickly learned that his task on Earth was far from completed. For all Emperor Yao's best efforts, the Middle Kingdom remained beset by such a catalogue of calamities that it seemed as though the world was returning to its primal state of chaos. Only Yi could put things to rights.

Yi's Heroic Missions

And so the bowman set off on a series of missions that rivalled the Labors of Hercules in their epic scope. First he had to deal with storms that were sweeping across China, uprooting crops and tearing down houses in their path. Using his divine power to travel on the wind, he tracked the gales back to their source, which turned out to be Taishan Mountain, far to the east. Yi then knew his adversary, for the mountain was the home of Fei Lian, the Count of the Winds, a fearsome spirit who generally took the form of a one-eyed bull with the tail of a serpent.

Using sheets to divert the wind, creating a corridor of calm air through which he could climb the mountain, Yi confronted the troublemaker in his lair. Fei Lian had shapeshifting powers, and at first Yi saw nothing but a seemingly innocuous sack standing in front of a cave's mouth when he reached the summit. For a moment the hero was fooled, but then he saw that the sack was straining at the seams under the pressure of the winds contained within it. Fitting an arrow to his bow, he fired at it. At once the bag burst asunder and in its place stood Fei Lian himself, bellowing.

A moonlit night in northern China evokes thoughts of eternity, for the Chinese myths related that it was on the moon that the white hare or rabbit resided that was believed to prepare the potion of immortality.

76

Seeing Yi reaching for another arrow, Fei Lian ran back into the cave, drawing his sword as he went. But Yi followed him and loosed a shaft that struck the wind god in the knee, dropping him to the ground. Wounded, he lost the will to fight, and grudgingly offered his submission.

With the threat of storms removed, Yi set off next to tame a river that had burst its banks. Suspecting that some turbulent river god was behind the trouble, he loosed an arrow at random into the swirling waters. Sure enough, the flood receded, revealing a white-garbed figure riding a white horse, surrounded by a dozen attendants. Before the spirit could escape, Yi fired again, wounding him in the eye, whereupon he whipped on his horse and fled, leaving his companions behind him.

Instantly, Yi took aim at the nearest figure. In the nick of time he realized his target was a girl and swung the bow so that the arrow whistled harmlessly through her hair. In gratitude she flung herself at his feet, and he learned that her name was Heng E and that she was a sister of the vanquished water god. Startled by her unworldly beauty, Yi asked her on the spot to be his wife, and Heng E accepted.

Yi's troubles were still far from over, for a plague of monstrous creatures had also chosen this time to maraud through the Middle Kingdom, spreading devastation in their wake. There was Chiseltooth, a fearsome giant with a single huge incisor protruding from the top of his mouth, which he used to rend his victims' flesh. A monstrous water serpent was disrupting the calm of Dongting Lake. The Windbird was a gigantic peacock that could cause storms merely by flapping its wings. All these menaces Yi dispatched with his bow, winning for himself from a grateful Emperor Yao the illustrious title of Marquis Pacifier of the Country.

An 8th-century Tang-dynasty tile showing a fierce creature that matches the description of Chiseltooth, a giant with a huge tooth used to rip his victims apart.

The Banishment of Yi

But if Yao was pleased with Yi's triumphs, Di Jun was not. Yi had killed the sun-birds, his errant children, instead of merely bringing them to heel; and for that the god could not easily forgive him. In his anger, he let it be known that he was banishing the bowman from the heavens; since Yi cared so much for the well-being of Earth, he could live there as a mere mortal.

The news left Yi dumbstruck. Searching for a way to regain what he had lost, he could think of only one possible course of action. He would travel to the palace of Xi Wang Mu, the Queen Mother of the West, in the Kunlun Mountains where Huang Di himself lived. There he would seek of her the elixir of immortality, distilled from

77

the wonderful peaches that grew nowhere but in her garden (see box below).

Yi set out at once. Using his magic power of flight he travelled westward to the fairy queen's palace, soaring effortlessly over the vast moat and the ring of fire that protected it. Once inside, he sought out Xi Wang Mu and humbly begged for the elixir, offering in return to serve her faithfully in any way she might choose. Pleased by his courtesy, the queen decided to favor his request. Knowing that he had great skill as an architect, she asked him to build her a summer palace in exchange for the drug.

For many months he labored, creating a residence fit for a goddess, its floors made of glass and its walls of translucent jade. When it was finished it pleased the queen, and in payment she handed

over a distillation of the elixir in the form of a tiny pill so potent that it glowed with a soft, evanescent light. Before Yi left, she warned him that he must not take it at once; to benefit from the potion's mystical powers, he must first prepare himself by prayer and meditation.

The Immortality of Heng E

Yi returned in triumph with his trophy. But on his arrival he found that Emperor Yao had urgent tasks waiting for him, and he had to leave home again without delay. Fearing that the pill might be stolen while he was away, he hid it in the rafters of his house.

He had hoped to be back before long, but he was mistaken. There were dangerous wild boars

Mystic Mistress of a Western Paradise

Xi Wang Mu, the Queen Mother of the West, was the fairy goddess of Chinese myth, and at one time people looked to her in hope of personal salvation. Yet there may have been fragments of historical truth behind all the tales of her magical fruit and golden palace.

According to the legends, Xi Wang Mu lived in a palace of pure gold set high on the summit of the Kunlun Mountains, mythical peaks in the west that may reflect distorted reports of the Hindu Kush. The walls that ringed it were 1,000 *li* (536 kilometers) in length and were topped with battlements of precious stones. There she lived surrounded by a celestial entourage that included the five Jade Fairy Maids. Whenever she left her paradise, she travelled on a white crane and used a flock of bluebirds as her messengers.

to be hunted down and a dragon that was terrorizing the Yellow River valley had to be confronted. Weeks dragged into months, and still his wife had no news of him.

Left on her own once more, Heng E pined for her absent husband. In her boredom she wandered the house alone, until one day her eye was caught by a strange light glowing from the roof-beams. Going to investigate, she found the magic pill wrapped in a silk covering.

She realized at once that the pill had special significance and she knew that she should leave it alone. But curiosity got the better of her. Taking it from its hiding place, she carried it downstairs to study it further. She was still holding it when, hearing a commotion outside, she stepped out of the house to find that, without warning, her husband

had at last come home. Panic-stricken, she swallowed the pill.

At once an extraordinary sense of lightness came over her. Escaping the pull of gravity, she found herself helplessly drawn upward. Yu saw her plight but was at a loss to know what was happening – until he noticed the pill's silk wrapping lying discarded on the ground. Too late, he tried to seize Heng E, but she was already well beyond his reach, soaring heavenward at an ever-faster rate.

She continued her ascent unimpeded until she reached the moon. It proved a desolate place, with no vegetation but a cassia tree. The only living things there were the white hare that the Chinese, like other peoples around the world, see in the markings on the moon's face, and the

In the palace gardens grew the Peaches of Immortality, mystical fruit that took 3,000 years to grow and a further 3,000 to ripen. Whenever one of the fruit matured, the goddess served it as the centerpiece of a feast whose other courses included monkeys' lips, dragons' liver and phoenix marrow. Guests were entertained by music from invisible instruments and songs from fairy tongues.

For a time around the end of the first millennium BCE, a cult formed around the queen and her western paradise, though before long it was supplanted by the greater attractions of the Daoist and Buddhist heavens. Yet in the earliest references the Queen Mother of the West was treated not so much as savior or goddess as a real-life ruler of some unidentified western state. According to a history of the

Zhou dynasty, written in the second century BCE, she is said to have received the Emperor Mu Wang in 985 BCE at a place called the Jewel Lake. Possibly it was that evocative place-name that inspired the later fantasies of the poets.

The gathering of the immortals at the golden palace of Xi Wang Mu by the banks of the Jewel Lake.

The moon (*left*) and the sun (*right*) from an 11th-century handscroll, personified as female and male respectively. In the story of Yi and Heng E, Yi represented the warm male principle of yang and resided accordingly in the palace of the sun, while Heng E represented the female principle of yin and lived in the palace of great cold, situated on the moon. Thus, natural and cosmic balance occurred.

heard his story in silence, then told him the gods' judgement on his actions. They had taken pity on him for his great labors on the Earthly sphere and the misfortunes that had afflicted him in return. They had decided that he should take his place again in their own ranks, only now he would occupy the palace of the sun. In so doing, he would lend it a male, yang presence to counterbalance the yin of Heng E's residence on the moon.

As Yi was leaving, the immortal handed him a leaving gift. It was a small red cake inscribed with a lunar talisman. It would, he was told, give him the power to visit Heng E, though she would never be able to come to him. That is why, Chinese people used to say, the light of the sun illuminates the moon but the moon cannot light up the sun.

So Yi took up his heavenly residence, relying on the experience of the sole surviving sun-bird to keep the orb moving on its diurnal course. It was not long before he first made use of the immortal's gift to visit his wife, who received him with rapture after her long spell of solitude. The two agreed that he should in future call on the fifteenth day of every lunar cycle. And so he still does, bringing yin and yang together to make the moon shine with an extra brilliance in the night sky at that time.

three-legged toad that was believed to devour it during eclipses.

And there she stayed, cursed with an immortality she had never wanted. In later times, she would be worshipped by the Chinese as Chang E, the Moon Goddess, and people would think sadly of her isolation as they gazed at its brightly shining orb on frosty winter evenings. (Her name was changed officially in *c.*2 BCE because Heng E broke a taboo concerning the emperor's own name.)

Yet she was not forgotten by her husband Yi. He sought in vain for a way to follow her up into the highest heavens, and finally decided to visit Xi Wang Mu's consort, a mighty being known as the King Father of the East. The immortal king

The Death of Yi

According to some accounts, Yi never regained immortality after his wife took the elixir of life. Instead, the great archer finally fell victim to the jealousy of a human rival he had chosen to befriend.

Feng Meng's skill at archery was surpassed only by that of Yi himself. Yi did his best to encourage the young hunter, teaching him the finer points of the bowman's art: how not to blink when aiming, the special skill of learning to see small objects as if they were large.

Under Yi's tuition, Feng Meng's talent blossomed. Soon he began to consider himself a rival even for his divine master. One day he challenged Yi to a shooting contest, taking aim at a flight of geese high up in the sky.

In an instant he had shot down three of the birds as they flew in line, each one with an arrow through the head. Before Yi could draw, the rest of the flock scattered across the skies, creating a seemingly impossible target. Even so, Yi brought down another trio just as neatly as his pupil, convincing Feng Meng that he would never outdo him.

In his bitterness, the hunter planned to kill Yi, knowing him to be now as mortal as any other man. Taking cover in a forest, he sought to ambush him, but each time that he sent an arrow whistling through the air, Yi countered with another that struck its shaft in mid-flight.

Thwarted at bowmanship, the assassin resorted to cruder methods to achieve his goal. Accompanying the unsuspecting Yi on a hunting trip, he waited until his companion had set aside his bow to pick up a bird that he had downed. Then he leaped upon him, bludgeoning him to death with the peachwood rod he used to carry home the game.

The Family Trials of Young Shun

Plotted against by a wicked stepmother with a son of her own, Shun never disowned his unjust family. His story became known to all Chinese as the first of the twenty-four examples of filial piety that taught respectful behavior toward parents.

Shun was still young when his mother died. After mourning her for three years, his father Gu Sou told the lad that he planned to remarry. Shun expressed his delight, promising to love the new wife as dearly as if she were his own mother. But the stepmother did not reciprocate, aiming to secure all Gu Sou's affections for her son, Xiang.

One day the father announced that he was going away on business. Shun – by now a young man – was left in charge of the household while he was gone, and his stepmother saw a chance to undermine him in Gu Sou's esteem. When word came that her husband was on his way home, she took a hairpin and drove it hard into her own heel.

Gu Sou returned to find her nursing her foot. When he asked what had happened, she claimed Shun had abused his father's absence to mistreat her shamelessly. As a final indignity he had thrown her onto a heap of thorns when she had been out in the orchard picking peaches.

Gu Sou was outraged by the accusation, and immediately demanded an explanation from his son. Shun knew that his stepmother had made up the story, yet through filial piety he was unwilling

A 12th-century painting showing an example of filial piety. Xiao, or the obligations owed to parents by their children, was a very important concept in Chinese thought and culture.

to defend himself and expose her as a liar. So he heard his father's recriminations in silence.

In punishment his father beat him until his back was raw. Shun accepted the blows uncomplainingly. But the gods, who watch over dutiful children, saw the injustice that had been done. They healed his wounds miraculously, and in a matter of hours no sign of the thrashing could be seen.

Shun's forbearance, and his unexpected recovery, only increased his stepmother's malice. She complained that Shun had spent the time his father was away in the wineshop, squandering family money among drunkards. Worse, he had sold off fields and orchards, giving the money to sorcerers to teach him black arts. For proof, she said, Gu Sou had only to consider the unnatural way his son's back had healed. Gu Sou was deceived by her lies. In a rage, he vowed to punish his son in any way his wife thought fit.

The evil woman bided her time for a couple of days, then came to him with a plan. Shun, she suggested, should be sent to repair a tumbledown barn on their property. Once he was up in the loft, they should shut the doors and set fire to the building, leaving him to die. Convinced by now that his son was a wastrel who would ruin them all, Gu Sou reluctantly agreed.

But Shun suspected something was afoot, and thoughtfully took two large-brimmed hats with him. As soon as the flames started to spread, he leaped from an upper window, using the hats as parachutes to break his fall.

Furious at his escape, the stepmother thought up a new ruse to be rid of him. This time Shun was asked to clear a rubble-clogged well. No sooner had he climbed in than the stepmother and her son blocked the top with a giant boulder.

The peach provides the motif for this Ming-dynasty vase. It was while she worked in her peach orchard that Shun's stepmother claimed he had injured her.

Shun's situation was desperate, but the gods once more came to his aid, spiriting him to safety on a neighbor's farm. Realizing his life would be in jeopardy if he returned home, he went instead to a wilderness region and cleared a plot of land to farm. There he prospered, but his family was not so lucky. His father's sight failed, and without a breadwinner their fortunes foundered.

Years passed and a drought struck the land, but Shun, with the gods' protection, still managed to bring in a good crop. Curious to know how his family was faring, he took some rice to a market near their home, hoping to hear news of them.

As it happened, they had been reduced to abject poverty. The stepmother had also come to market, but only to barter a wretched bundle of firewood. Failing to recognize Shun, she approached him with the few coins it raised to buy rice. She was astonished to receive twice what she had expected – and the stallholder, as if by accident, slipped the money she had given him into the bag as well.

When Gu Sou heard of her good fortune, a wild notion entered his head. Could the kindly stranger be Shun, whom he had thought dead? The others poured scorn on the idea but, undeterred, he insisted on going to find out for himself.

As soon as the blind man heard Shun's voice, he recognized his child and the two fell into one another's arms and embraced. At first Gu Sou wanted to punish his wife for leading him astray, but Shun would have none of it. The stepmother tearfully expressed her repentance, and through Shun's exemplary filial piety and forbearance, the dislocated family were finally reconciled. Word of Shun's behavior eventually reached Emperor Yao himself and the dutiful son found his name put forward for high office.

Gun and the Swelling Soil

In Yao's day, floods as well as fire threatened the Middle Kingdom. The emperor sought help from Heaven in the form of Gun, who solved the flooding but outraged his grandfather, Huang Di, in the process.

While Shun was turning the tables on his wicked stepmother, the Emperor Yao was still struggling with the elements, which threatened to overwhelm the order he had fought so hard to impose. When fire had menaced the land, Di Jun had sent Yi to his assistance. Now the threat came from floods.

This time Yao turned for help to a divinity named Four Mountains, guardian of the four quarters of the universe. The spirit directed him to an immortal named Gun, a grandson of Huang Di, the Yellow Emperor, who now ruled the heavens.

Gun was only too pleased to help. He had compassion for the human race, and had watched the disasters afflicting them with sorrow. But he was at a loss to know how to set about the task until he had a strange encounter with two odd spirit beings. One took the shape of a black tortoise, the other that of a horned owl.

The curious couple waylaid him and asked him why he looked so worried. When he explained his problem, they assured him there was an easy way to halt the flooding: all he needed was a handful of Swelling Soil.

Asked what that was, they explained that it was a magical substance in the possession of his grandfather Huang Di. Placed anywhere on Earth, it would go on growing until told to stop. Its absorbent qualities would soak up the floodwaters in no time.

Gun objected that Huang Di, as Lord of Heaven, must have ordained the flooding and would never let him have the soil. In that case, they said, he would have to steal it. He asked them how, and they whispered in his ear a secret so closely guarded that it has never been revealed.

Following their instructions, Gun indeed managed to procure some of the magical soil, and he lost no time in trying it out. It was quite as effective as the couple had claimed. A pea-sized fragment, dropped onto a flooded plain, would grow until it had soaked up all the waters under a fresh and fertile covering of topsoil. Then, at a word of command, the swelling would stop.

Slowly life began to return to normal in Yao's kingdom. People who had taken refuge in the mountains returned to the reclaimed land eager to build their lives afresh. Fresh hope dawned across the country.

But one observer looking down from Heaven was far from pleased. Huang Di saw that his authority had been challenged, and with divine omniscience knew at once who was responsible for the offense. Terrible in his outraged majesty, the deity deputed the task of punishing the troublemaker to the fearsome Jurong, Spirit of Fire and executioner of all who fell foul of the gods.

In his heart of hearts Gun knew the fate that awaited him, yet he still did all in his power to escape. For nine years he kept his pursuer at bay. He fled to the farthermost ends of the Earth but could not shake off the avenging spirit. It was at Feather Mountain in the far north that Jurong finally tracked him down. There in the icy wastes the avenger slew him.

Yet though Gun was dead, robbed of his immortality by Huang Di's command, a remarkable thing happened. His body did not decompose. It remained where it had fallen, as though preserved by the ice, yet even so new life stirred within it. For a child was growing inside Gun, and after three years it was ready to emerge. Gun's belly split open, and from it came Yu – a future emperor and the man who would finally quell the floods that his father had given his life to tame.

An Ever-Present Threat

Floods were a constant danger in early China, and their central role in myth reflects their overriding importance in real life. Chinese civilization developed in the lands watered by the Yellow River, a treacherous life-giver estimated to have burst its banks 1,500 times in the past 3,000 years.

While the inundations leave a rich layer of silt that ensures the fertility of the region, they also bring heartache, taking a toll of millions of lives and winning for the river the name of "China's sorrow." Over the millennia the inhabitants of the surrounding floodplain have fought to combat the torrent by building dikes to contain the river's flow. Today the river is held in check by ramparts as much as thirty meters wide at the base and fifteen meters high.

Inevitably, the unceasing labor required to channel the river and divert its waters to productive use found a reflection in myth. Legendary heroes like Gun and Yu personify the efforts of generations of early rulers to tame the inundations.

One interesting result is that China's flood myths have little in common with the Deluge stories familiar from the Bible and elsewhere; perhaps because of the very familiarity of the tragedy, they present the disaster as a natural catastrophe rather than as divine judgement on a sinful world.

Floods have been both a curse and a blessing for China, and attempts to harness and control the waters of the major rivers have permeated China's mythology and recorded history. The development of skillful wet-rice agriculture (*seen below*) in the lower Yangtzi basin – with canals built to distribute it – made the country self-sufficient but left many people vulnerable to flooding.

Yao Finds an Heir

Hard-pressed to find an heir to succeed him, the Emperor Yao finally settled on Shun. The elevation of the humbly born farmer to the highest office in the land was testament indeed to the worthiness of virtue, one of the traditional Five Blessings.

Worn down by his unceasing struggle against the elements, Yao was tired. He needed a right-hand man to help him battle the floods. In the back of his mind, too, was the search for a an heir to succeed him, for he already knew that his son Dan Zhu (see box opposite) was not up to the job.

So he called a grand council and asked the wise men of the realm to suggest a suitable candidate. Their deliberations were recorded for posterity in the *Book of History*. Various names were put forward, but all were rejected for different reasons. "He's all talk" the Emperor complained of one contender; "he doesn't obey orders" of another.

Finally, in despair, Yao asked for a fresh suggestion, adding, "It doesn't matter whether he's a gentleman or not, just so long as his virtue is adequate." At once several recommended Shun. Yao replied that he had heard the name, but asked to know more of him. He listened to the tale of Shun's tribulations in silence, then said bluntly, "I will try him."

And so Shun, the humble farmer, was summoned to court, and to his amazement was offered high office. At first he protested that he was unworthy of the honor, but the emperor insisted. But he also made it clear that Shun was on trial, and he would face instant dismissal if he proved unfit for the responsibilities placed upon him.

For three years Yao watched the young man's every action. He devised difficult challenges to test his mettle, sending him on his own deep into remote forest fastnesses to see if he could survive unscathed. Shun overcame every danger, and the emperor's admiration for him grew steadily. Eventually he paid him the

Wooden Ming-dynasty figure of an aged Chinese dignitary wearing full robes and an official's hat. Such men offered advice in court and wielded considerable influence; indeed, it was such people who proposed Shun to Yao.

The Preposterous Dan Zhu

Emperor Yao chose not to pass on his throne to his son Dan Zhu, who for later generations became the archetype of the irresponsible heir unfit to inherit high office.

Dan Zhu's selfishness and insensitivity knew no bounds. He loved to go on boat trips even when drought gripped the kingdom, forcing sweating minions to carry the craft along the dried-up riverbeds. When his father taught him chess to keep him harmlessly occupied, he chose to play it in the most extravagant way, planting an entire plain in a checkerboard pattern of groves and open spaces and using live rhinoceroses and elephants to serve as the thirty-two pieces.

In time his excesses so alienated Yao that the emperor determined to banish him to the far south. There the angry prince stirred up trouble, raising the flag of revolt among disaffected border tribes. But he had no talent as a military leader, and soon he and his supporters were fleeing for their lives from the emperor's armies, halting only when they reached the sea. There, in his despair, Dan Zhu

killed himself by leaping into the waters. But it was not the end of him, for his spirit took the form of a bird called the zhu, shaped like an owl but with human hands. In later times it showed itself only in lands that were badly governed, its appearance a sure sign that high officials were about to be dismissed.

ultimate compliment of giving him two of his own daughters in marriage.

Yao's health was failing, but he knew that at last he had found a man in whom he could have confidence. Finally he summoned him to the audience chamber before all the dignitaries of the realm. "Approach, Shun," he said, stepping down from the throne to greet him. "For three years I have compared your deeds with your words, and you do what you say. Ascend the Dragon Seat!"

The entire court bowed low as Shun stepped up, first to reign jointly with Yao as regent and later, when the old emperor died, to rule alone. He proved a fit successor in every way, showing the same virtue and wisdom. And even in his new eminence, he never forgot his duty to his family, conferring on his stepbrother Xiang a high position at the court. Xiang proved so grateful for the mercy shown to him that he forgot all his earlier grudges and became a most loyal subject.

Yu the Flood-Tamer

Shun inherited Yao's responsibilities along with his office, and the most pressing of these was the need to combat the floods that were still ravaging the countryside. For help in mastering them, he turned to Gun's son Yu.

Calling together his ministers, he asked if they could recommend a man capable of combating the threat. Unanimously they recommended Yu, a young man eager to complete the job that his father Gun had so bravely started.

On receiving the imperial commission, Yu knew that he could accomplish it only with the aid of the Swelling Soil. To avoid making his father's mistake, he went humbly to Huang Di and asked to use it with his permission. Pleased by his submissive manner, the god gave his consent, stipulating that Yu could have as much of the soil as could be carried on the back of a tortoise – perhaps the same beast that had given such dangerous advice to Gun.

Given the soil's amazing properties, it was more than Yu needed, and he set to work at once. He soon discovered that the floods afflicting the Middle Kingdom were unusual in that much of the water came not from the skies but from below the earth, welling up from underground watercourses. To staunch the springs, Yu had repeatedly to dive into the waters and fix a stopper of the

A Song-dynasty portrait of Yu, who, the Chinese characters declare on the painting, "worked tirelessly for the country so that nobody among his people was without grain . . . He was never boastful yet none has equalled his glory."

Swelling Soil in the gap. It was exhausting work, for the subterranean aquifer seemed almost limitless. Some people equated it with the Yellow Springs, the underground stream by which the sun was thought to travel eastward back to the Fu Shan tree every night.

Even so, Yu labored on, never losing heart, and after a time it seemed that he was winning the battle. Then disturbing news started to arrive from lands that he had already cleared. Mysteriously, the waters were rising again. Someone or something was undoing the work that he had so laboriously accomplished.

Yu soon learned that his enemy was none other than Gong Gong, the Spirit of the Waters, who in earlier times had tilted all China by bumping into Buzhou Mountain. Furious to see the floods receding, he was following in Yu's footsteps in an attempt to undo everything the hero had achieved.

Yu realized that the only response was war, so he summoned all the other spirits to Mount Kuai Ji in southeastern China to do battle.

Shun's Ministers

Later emperors looked back to Yao's heir as a model monarch, noting Confucius's dictum that, "Shun had five ministers and all that is under Heaven was well ruled."

According to the *Book of History*, Shun called together the chief personages of the land after Emperor Yao's death to inquire who could best help him govern the kingdom. One of the men they recommended, Gao Yao, had already made his reputation as a law officer in the previous reign. A man named Yi was made responsible for forests and wilderness areas, and he set about burning off scrub to open up new land for cultivation. Prince Jie – the name means "millet" – was delegated to teach the people the use of the different types of grain. A certain Xie was appointed Public Instructor, with the duty of familiarizing Shun's subjects with the Five Precepts governing correct behavior between parents and children, rulers and subjects, friends and associates, masters and servants and husbands and wives. Above them all, "to transact the emperor's affairs," he appointed a man who was to become a legend in his own right – the mighty Yu (see pages 90–95).

A 16th-century ceramic piece by Wan Li showing a local magistrate at work.

Seeing the huge host arrayed against him, Gong Gong took flight and caused Yu no further trouble. At last the flood-tamer could devote himself single-mindedly to the task that Shun had given him. To give him extra encouragement, the emperor announced that henceforward Yu would serve as his regent, acting as joint ruler of the Middle Kingdom.

After stopping up all the larger springs, Yu tried a new tactic to drain off the remaining surface water. Instead of building dikes to contain the flooding, he started digging channels to let the overflow run off into rivers and the sea. To help him, he called on the assistance of a white dragon whose tail served as a gigantic hoe, gouging out furrows that helped to drain the waters.

Sometimes Yu's hydrological projects involved tunnelling through mountains, and in the course of one such venture – the hollowing out of Longmen, the Dragon Gate – the hero had an extraordinary encounter. His task took him into a cavern that led deep into a mountainside, far from the sunlight and the noises of the outside world. As he moved onward into the black stillness, he could make out a faint glow coming from the innermost heart of the cavern. Advancing cautiously with a drawn sword in his hand, he found himself in the presence of a bizarre figure, with the head of a man joined to a serpent's body.

Reverently Yu dropped to his knees, for he recognized the mighty Fu Xi. The god addressed him in measured tones, expressing satisfaction with the work he had done and encouraging him to see it through to the end. But that would not be the end of his labors, Fu Xi added, for he was to be the man who would finally bring political order to the Middle Kingdom. To help him with the task, the god passed him two jade tablets that would, he said, help him to measure and map the kingdom. Given heart by this divine endorsement, Yu resumed his labors with fresh vigor, and finally, after thirteen years, the task was completed.

Yu and the Tragic Marriage

A strange tale bearing echoes of primitive religion told how Yu found a bride through a vision, only to lose her tragically as a result of exercising his supernatural, shapeshifting powers when engaged in a dangerous and demanding task.

For all his unremitting labors, Yu nonetheless found the time to get married, and he did so in an unexpected way. He had reached the age of thirty, regarded in later times by disciples of Confucius as the correct age for a man to think of taking a wife. Some such thought was in his own mind one day when he happened to spot an animal running out of cover not far away. He got a clear view of it and saw that it was a white fox with nine tails – a famously propitious omen. At once the words of a popular folksong flashed into his head:

If a nine-tailed fox should pass you by
A royal crown before you lies.
Marry a girl from Tushan hill
A golden throne your heirs will fill.

Yu needed no more encouragement. He travelled at once to the southern district where the hill of Tushan lay, and found that the local headman had a daughter of marriageable age named Nü Jiao. The hero asked to see her, and found her polite and comely. On the spot he asked for her hand in marriage, and she and her father were both delighted to agree.

Yet for Nü Jiao the marriage was not to be a happy one. She had to leave her home and her loved ones to take up residence with her husband, only to find that she almost never saw him, for he was constantly travelling. Even so, she found herself pregnant after one of their rare nights together. In her loneliness, she insisted on accompanying him on his next journey, even though he did his best to persuade her against the idea.

As it happened, he and his men were tunnelling at the time among the precipices of the Huanyuan Mountains of Zhejiang Province. It was

hard labor, and each day Yu rose before dawn to urge it forward. His wife longed to see him at work, but he enjoined her in the strictest terms never to follow him.

Eventually the prohibition started to irk Nü Jiao, who could see no good reason why she should not see for herself exactly what he got up

to each day. And so a morning came when she decided to ignore his warnings. Alone, she headed into the mountains along the track her husband regularly took.

What Nü Jiao did not know was that Yu, who had inherited shapeshifting powers from his divine father, Gun, had been taking the form of a giant bear to tunnel through the mountain. Transformed, he would use his massive paws to tear away the soil. So when his wife tracked him down to the cave in which he was working, she was confronted not by the man she loved but by a gigantic and fearsome beast that reared on its hind legs and roared in fury at the sight of an intruder trespassing in its lair.

Nü Jiao fled in terror. In a flash Yu changed into human form and pursued her, but it only confused and frightened her more. She fled all the way to the foot of Songgao Mountain, where in her panic she halted and was turned to stone.

Yu stopped, baffled and afraid, and then in anguish howled, "Give me my son!" Somehow his words must have reached Nü Jiao, for the rock split apart to reveal a living baby boy. Reverently Yu carried him to safety. Named Qi, "cracked open," the child would eventually rule over China as the second emperor of the Xia dynasty.

An early 19th-century watercolor on silk of the bride's party arriving at the bridegroom's house, her new home.

Yu Mounts the Dragon Throne

As a reward for his heroic labors, the dying Shun named Yu as his heir. As emperor, the flood-tamer continued the great tradition of his sainted predecessors, starting China's first dynasty, the Xia, and a pattern of hereditary monarchy that lasted for millennia.

Shun reigned for many peaceful years, but eventually his strength began to ebb and he knew that he was not much longer for this world. It was time to choose his successor and, as expected, he confirmed that it would be his faithful regent Yu. He passed on some advice to his successor that the *Book of History* faithfully recorded: "Be reverent. Behave carefully on the throne that you will occupy, and respectfully cultivate the virtue expected of you." Then the wise old emperor died.

For three years Yu observed an official period of mourning for his predecessor, deified once he had passed over into the spirit world. Then he flung himself energetically into the task of bringing order that Fu Xi had predicted for him.

Yu soon found a use for the jade tablets that Fu Xi had presented to him, passing them on to two officials delegated to measure the entire known world. One travelled from north to south and the other from east to west, and when they came back to court they each reported an identical distance: 233,500 *li* and 75 paces, or approximately 125,250 kilometers. This confirmed the ancient Chinese view that the world was square.

An undated scroll depicting the building of dikes during the reign of Kangxi in the mid-17th century. Dikes efficiently complemented channels as a means of controlling floodwaters, and during Yu's reign some spectacular drainage tunnels were built through the Wu Shan Mountains in Sichuan.

Benevolent Monsters

Unlike their malign counterparts in European tradition, Chinese dragons were usually regarded as auspicious beasts.

A detail of a 19th-century ceramic dragon spouting water from high in the clouds, reflecting the dragon's traditional role as a bringer of rain.

In Chinese myth, dragons seem to have had their origins as rain deities, and the connection with water always remained strong. They were usually thought of as living in lakes and rivers; some authorities also think they had a connection with the Yellow Springs, the underground stream through which the sun was held to travel in the nighttime hours. They were regularly invoked in time of drought, and the Dragon Dance that is still performed at Chinese New Year festivities today originated as a ritual designed to encourage rain.

Though they were powerful creatures capable of doing great harm, dragons were generally portrayed as protectors, guarding treasure, or even Heaven itself, keeping watch over waterways and the clouds and winds. Their image of beneficent power was appreciated by China's rulers, who appropriated the dragon as an imperial symbol.

Yu himself resumed the peripatetic lifestyle he had known as the flood-tamer, journeying constantly to every quarter of his realm. On his travels he saw many wonders. One was Yuqiang, who lived at the northernmost limit of the world. God of the ocean wind, he was said to have a bird's body with a human face, and it was he whom the Ruler of Heaven had delegated to moor the floating Island of Immortals to a fixed position in the Eastern Sea.

Much of Yu's time now was spent on problems of administration as he strove to provide a framework of just government for a land still reeling from its long history of natural catastrophe. He ordered a census of the entire population and a survey of the fields. Officials were sent out to check all the openings through which underground springs had bubbled up in the time of floods. They listed almost a quarter of a million sizeable vents, all of which were checked to confirm that they were adequately blocked up. But the smaller outlets, less than eight paces across, were innumerable, and it was considered impractical to fill them all. That, ancient writers claimed, was why small-scale flooding continued in China to their day, even though cataclysmic inundations no longer occurred as they did in Shun's time.

As part of a general reorganization, Yu divided the Middle Kingdom into nine separate provinces, each with its own governor and an appointed tribute of lacqueurs and silks. Ores sent from the regions were used to make nine magnificent tripod cauldrons, each decorated with insignia representing the people and products of the relevant district. These vessels were passed down from ruler to ruler, becoming important symbols of imperial power.

It was said of the tripods that they increased in weight when China was well governed and grew lighter in times of bad rule. So when Yu passed them on to his son Qi, it took ninety oxen to move one, but in the last, decadent days of the Xia dynasty a single person could carry it away.

For all his successes, Yu remained profoundly humble, all too aware of the limitations of his achievement. On one occasion, while out riding he met a criminal in chains and is said to have burst into tears, protesting that the existence of crime in his kingdom was proof that his own virtue as a ruler was insufficient. On another occasion, he submissively sat through a homily from his chief minister, who reminded him of the duties of a good king – not to have preconceived notions, to listen to the views of all, to aid the helpless and support the poor. Listening to the list, Yu threw up his hands in despair, protesting "Only the Emperor Yao could maintain that standard" – to which the minister replied that Yu would not have been granted the Mandate of Heaven if his virtue had not been up to the job.

Yu Fights the Serpent with Nine Heads

Although peace had returned to the Middle Kingdom, threats still arose from time to time that required all Yu's old courage and initiative. One such occasion occurred late in his reign, when word reached him of a monstrous creature named Xiangyao that was ravaging an outlying district of his realm. It came as no surprise to learn that the scourge was an emissary of Yu's old enemy Gong Gong, sent to spread misery and desolation in the newly ordered lands.

The beast had a serpent's body and nine heads, each of which spat forth a venom so noxious that it laid waste all the land around. It was huge in size, and when at rest it wrapped itself round nine separate hills.

At first Yu hoped to take the creature by surprise, but he quickly realized the futility of that plan. Even as it rested, its heads were constantly in motion, scanning every point of the compass for food to eat or enemies to kill. For a time the old emperor was hard pressed to come up with a way of confronting it, but then he had a flash of inspiration. He realized he would once more need the services of an old ally, the Winged Dragon. They would ride together for a final time.

What Yu had noticed was that the serpent never looked upward, apparently assuming that no danger was to be expected from that source. So Yu mounted the dragon, sword in hand. Together the pair soared up and circled round until they were directly above their prey. Then they dropped almost vertically upon it as its reptilian eyes unsuspectingly scoured the horizon below.

Yu's sword flashed in the sunlight, and two heads were gone before the monster had time to react. Then it made a fight of it; its remaining heads bobbed and weaved like flails threshing grain. But the dragon was nimble and Yu's aim was unerring. As the final head was lopped off, the great body shook convulsively and lay still.

Yet the harm the beast caused did not die with it. From its mouths a steady flow of venom trickled, blighting the fields where they lay. Yu gave orders for the heads to be covered over with earth, but the poison in them found its way into the ground water, spreading to the land around.

The same thing happened when the remains were dug up and interred together in a single huge mound. Eventually the only solution proved to lie in burying them on an island in an artificial lake, whose waters served to soak up the remaining toxins and to insulate the neighboring district from their virulence.

Yu had reigned single-handedly for only eight years when he killed Xiangyao, but he sensed that his time was almost up. He decided to go on a final tour of his realm. It was on this trip that death came to him, suddenly but peacefully while he was visiting Kuai Ji Mountain where, many years earlier, he had summoned the spirit army to do battle with Gong Gong. His body was buried in a great cave on the mountainside that in later times would become a place of pilgrimage. The historian Sima Qian visited it as a young man in Han dynasty times more than 2,000 years after Yu's death, paying his respects to the hero as part of a grand tour of his country's antiquities.

It was Sima Qian too who reported that Yu nominated his chief minister, Bo Yi, to succeed him on the Dragon Throne, but that the lords of the land refused to accept his candidate. Instead they pledged allegiance to Yu's son Qi, thereby establishing the hereditary principle that was to survive in China through all its various dynasties. Qi duly took up office as the second ruler of the Xia dynasty; and the oppressive weight of the nine bronze cauldrons throughout his reign can be taken as evidence that he did his best to follow worthily in the footsteps of Yao, Shun and Yu.

A dramatically fierce-looking, serpent-like dragon, in gold thread, decorates this 17th-century kesi, or silk tapestry. The dragon is depicted with all the traditional elements: a reptile's scaly skin, a stag's horns, long feline whiskers and four claws (five signified an imperial symbol). There are clouds and waves too, connecting the dragon to both water and sky, its two principal domains.

The Fall of Dynasties

In China's moralistic view of history, dynasties collapsed when their rulers misbehaved. Just as the virtues of the Sage Kings promoted their subjects' well-being, so the wicked ways of two notorious tyrants guaranteed trouble and the Mandate of Heaven was withdrawn.

If the early histories are to be believed, the Xia dynasty took its course peacefully for almost 500 years through seventeen successive rulers. The last of these, however, was a tyrant who bled the people dry to cater to his own pleasures.

Jie would waste a fortune on a whim. One of his concubines liked the sound of tearing silk, so

bale after bale was shredded for her pleasure. And he was as cruel as he was extravagant. He once set tigers from the royal zoo free in a marketplace, simply for the pleasure of seeing the people running for their lives.

Unsurprisingly, he was much hated, and when Tang, the Lord of Shang, raised the standard of revolt against him, people flocked to join his cause. The defeated emperor fled south, where he died shortly afterward, a lonely exile dreaming of his lost powers.

The Shang dynasty brought China out of the era of myth and into history. Yet there was one Shang ruler about whom legends would accumulate, and once again he was the last of the line.

Zhou Xin was a despot in the mold of Jie. He was strong and he was intelligent, but it was said of him that, "With his eloquence he refuted good advice, and with his wit veiled his faults."

When one of his vassals, the Prince of Zhou, showed signs of discontent, Zhou Xin arrested him and took his son hostage. At a banquet one night, the emperor remarked drunkenly of the prince: "They say he's a wise man and knows many things. Do you think he'd be clever enough to recognize the taste of his own son?" Upon which, he gave orders for the son to be killed and boiled in a broth, which was duly served to his prisoner. Zhou Xin laughed uproariously when he heard that the prince had unsuspectingly drunk it.

This barbaric act was an error the emperor was to live to regret. The prince's heir, Wu, raised

A depiction of Emperor Wu by an unknown artist. Wu was the first ruler of the Zhou dynasty on whose behalf many gods had fought to overthrow the despotic regime of the last Shang emperor, Zhou Xin.

the standard of revolt, and rebels flocked to his side from across the kingdom. And according to the storytellers the Prince of Zhou had divine aid too, receiving the help of the gods of the rivers and the seas and the deities of wind and rain.

The two sides finally met at the decisive battle of Mu in 1027 BCE. Historians record that Zhou Xin's soldiers quickly turned tail and fled. In the myths, however, the Earthly struggle was accompanied by an epic combat, the Battle of Ten Thousand Spirits, in which gods joined the fray to rout the forces of evil in Heaven as on Earth.

The defeated Zhou Xin then made his way back to his palace, dressed himself up in his most splendid robes and set fire to the building.

In the centuries that followed, the fates of Jie and Zhou Xin became object lessons for philosophers and historians, illustrating the evils that descended on the kingdom when its rulers abandoned virtue for sensual delights. The two became the obverse of the Sage Kings, dire warnings to later generations whose fates showed all too graphically that the Mandate of Heaven could be withdrawn if sovereigns ruled without consent.

Zhou Xin the Shang Sadist

Zhou Xin was said to be intelligent, though in a highly perverse way. He satisfied his inquisitiveness with horrific experiments.

To judge from the stories, he had a particular interest in the workings of the human body – one that he indulged in a vicious manner. Seeing some peasants wading through a stream in mid-winter, he had their legs cut off so he could study the effects of the cold on their bone marrow. When his uncle, Prince Bi Gan, once reproved him for his failings, he replied, "You're said to be a sage, and I have heard that sages have seven openings in the heart" – whereupon he ordered that the prince be killed and cut open so that he could check if the claim was true.

A CITY OF SYMBOLS

For the last five centuries of imperial rule, the hub of Earthly power was a walled complex of residences and audience chambers in the heart of Beijing's inner city. There resided China's emperor, the occupant of the oldest throne in the world, the Son of Heaven and the "Lord of 10,000 Years" with a divine right to rule known as the Heavenly Mandate. Following the principles of geomancy, the Forbidden City was laid out on a north-south axis with its four gates oriented to the cardinal points of the compass. Lined up in the center were the great ceremonial buildings: the Hall of Supreme Harmony, from which state edicts were promulgated; the Hall of Perfect Harmony, where the throne stood; and the Hall of Protective Harmony, in which scholars and diplomats were received. In each, care was taken to ensure that the emperor always sat facing south, a propitious direction associated with the yang principle. The layout of the complex reflected ancient Chinese ideas that the world was square, with China itself – the Middle Kingdom – at its sacred center.

Throughout the buildings and court-yards of the Forbidden City, animal symbols abounded in the form of cranes, lions, turtles and other beasts, many of them designed to protect the emperor and his entourage from evil spirits. One, however, dominated: the dragon, the symbol of authority, fertility, goodness and strength and the benevolent bringer of wealth and good fortune, was omnipresent. The emperor occupied the Dragon Throne, wore Dragon Robes and even slept in the Dragon Bed. The ordinary people of China sometimes referred to themselves as Children of the Dragon. In addition to the animals, there was an important use of color: azure, red, yellow, white and black constituted the Five Colors. Red and yellow were particularly prominent in the Forbidden City. The temples and palaces were red to bring good fortune, for it is the color associated with summer, fire and the south; while many of the roof tiles were glazed yellow, symbolic of earth, and the imperial shade that represented the Middle Kingdom.

Above: A painting on silk of the city by Zhu Bang. Only senior figures could enter the three-arched Meridian Gate, whereupon they crossed one of five bridges, numbered for their symbolism.

Top left: A bronze dragon, the animal most associated with imperial power.

Left: The Hall of Supreme Harmony, or Tai He Dian, with its "bird-wing" roof, was where the emperor celebrated the New Year and the winter solstice, appointed generals and read out the names of those who had passed their exams to gain entry to the civil service.

Above: The Forbidden City was built by Yongle, the third Ming emperor, in the 15th century, but for much of its existence the Manchu Qing dynasty reigned there. This painting shows officials prostrating themselves before the emperor. The Qings were a non-Chinese people from the north and although the court remained a place of splendor and tradition during the dynasty's 250-year existence, China itself became much weaker compared to the outside world. The bronze tripod incense burners symbolized imperial rule; there was one to represent every province of China.

Above: The dragon is the essence of male yang, and this motif relief is from one of the white marble passageways that bisect the steps and access ramps of the Forbidden City. The emperor was carried up and down above it by attendants on the steps at either side.

Below: A 19th-century woman's headdress offers a suggestion of courtly splendor. Pearls were a distillation of the essence of the moon and female yin, and they also represented imperial treasure. The words read: "Receive Heaven's Mandate."

Left: A tortoise symbolized wisdom and longevity, peace and stability. It represented the cardinal direction of north and it is said that its shell betokened the vault of the universe. The myths say that the tortoise emerged from the Luo River bearing on its shell the Luo Shu mystic diagrams that inspired Fu Xi. Bronze tortoise statues were situated in front of the Hall of Supreme Harmony and the Palace of Heavenly Purity.

MATTERS OF FAITH

Daoism and Buddhism represent the popular face of Chinese religion. While intellectuals and administrators looked to Confucius for a worldview stressing social responsibility and civic duty, the mass of the people wanted faiths that more directly addressed their immediate needs. Facing a daily struggle to make a living, they sought beliefs that promised help in time of trouble and that held out the possibility of salvation in the years to come. For them the innumerable divinities of the Daoist and Buddhist faiths – many of them shared between the two – gave the workings of impersonal destiny a recognizable face. However fearsome the gods might sometimes seem, they could always be placated by ritual observations that gave the individual some sense of control over an otherwise unfathomable world.

Of the two, Daoism was the native growth, beginning in the fourth century BCE as a mystical philosophy that stressed the importance of spontaneity over planned activity and of direct experience against rational thought. By advocating the unconscious as opposed to the conscious mind, it served to counterbalance the rationalism of Confucianism.

It took half a millennium for this esoteric doctrine to develop into an organized religion. Along the way it attracted a host of ancient superstitions and folk beliefs largely unconnected with its intellectual origins. Some of this lore came from the wu shamans, the guardians of China's oldest religious traditions. To it the priests added an organizational framework and the practicing of a set of spiritual disciplines intended to help devotees conquer death by attaining inner perfection.

Buddhism arrived in China along the Silk Road about the time that Daoism was establishing itself as an organized faith, and it too soon had adherents all over the country. It brought in similar mystical concerns and a fresh pantheon of gods, plus a monastic tradition that the Daoists would later copy.

Yet for all their independent histories, the two faiths ultimately came together in the popular mind. Few Chinese ever devoted themselves single-mindedly to one or the other; most borrowed gods and rituals promiscuously from both, and their myths too reflect this cultural melting pot. The world of gods and spirits was crowded, and it knew no borders.

Opposite: An 18th-century *kesi*, or silk tapestry, depicting some of the central Daoist figures in paradise. Atop the cloud is Xi Wang Mu, Queen Mother of the West; on the balcony nearest are three star gods and the Eight Immortals.

Left: A carved ivory Lohan representing one of the disciples of the Buddha. The Lohan, or Arhat, were subsequently reflected in the Eight Immortals of Daoism.

103

A Bureaucracy of Gods

Inheriting China's popular religious traditions, the Daoists organized its thousands of gods into a heavenly version of imperial rule on Earth – complete with a God of Examinations and a Ministry of Thunder.

The founders of Daoism recognized no gods at all. The *Dao De Jing* and the *Zhuangzi* spoke only of the Dao itself, the ineffable wellspring of all being. The Dao, they said, had no name, for the very act of naming involved differentiation while it was in everything as the primal force. The individual's goal was to live in tune with the Dao, which meant learning to go with the grain of the physical world rather than trying to impose a pattern on it.

In practice, Daoism favored spontaneity over planning, the unconscious over the conscious mind. Politically, it stood for laissez-faire government as opposed to state intervention; the highest ambition of a ruler should be not to be seen to be governing. Daoist thinkers stressed the importance of yielding ground in order to advance and sang the praises of non-interference and inactivity.

These concepts quickly struck a chord in China, serving to complement the activist, socially minded views of Confucius. While Confucianism appealed to the rational, organizing instincts, Daoism became a magnet for darker, more instinctive forces, touching a vein of native mysticism.

In time too it became the mouthpiece of popular religion. Since time immemorial, the mass of the Chinese people had worshipped a multiplicity of gods, some of the soil, others of the elements, many more tied to a specific locality. To this day no one has ever tried to catalogue all these multifarious deities, which varied from place to place.

The Examination God

The crowded Chinese pantheon had many niches. One of its most popular denizens was the deity who supervised success in examinations.

Kui Xing was the most brilliant scholar of his day, but, unfortunately, he was also physically repulsive. When he took the examinations for entry into the imperial civil service, he got the highest marks. Custom demanded that, as top scholar, he should receive a golden rose from the hand of the emperor himself. But the ruler took one look at Kui Xing's ugly face and refused to present it.

The young man was devastated. In his distress, he went to the coast and flung himself into the sea, intending to kill himself. But a strange beast – some say it was a fish, others a turtle – rose from beneath the waves and carried him to safety. Subsequently he ascended to

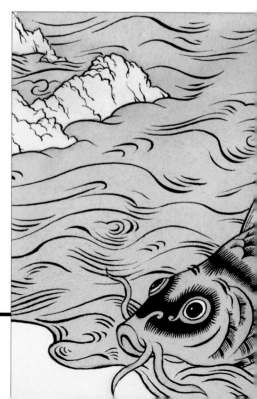

A Divine Hierarchy

The Daoists inherited this teeming mass of gods and set about organizing them. They modelled the divine hierarchy directly on the political world they knew, providing Heaven with an emperor, ministers and minor officials just like China itself.

At the pinnacle of power was Yu Di, the Jade Emperor. Although he was a relative late-comer, dating only from the eleventh century CE, he drew on the authority of earlier celestial rulers. These included Shangdi, from 2,000 years earlier, and Tian or "Heaven", the less personalized concept of supreme godhead worshipped from the Zhou era.

Yu Di had lived on Earth before attaining perfection as a god. Long childless, his royal parents had asked the priests to pray that they might have a son. Next night the deified sage Laozi appeared to the queen in a dream, carrying a baby in his arms, and she subsequently found she was pregnant with the infant Yu. He later inherited the throne, but gave it up to follow a contemplative life. Attaining perfection, he devoted the rest of his time on Earth to healing the sick.

His cult dated from the reign of the Song emperor Zhen Zong, who seems to have introduced it as a way of boosting his own standing following a humiliating military defeat. Although all sectors of Chinese society accepted the new supreme god, he was always more popular in court circles than among the public at large. For the most part it was only the monarch himself who prayed directly to Yu Di, making sacrifices to him annually at the Altar of Heaven in Beijing. Just as on Earth most people considered themselves too lowly to send a petition to the emperor in person, so on the divine plane they preferred to address themselves to some intermediary god.

There was plenty of choice, for beneath the Jade Emperor was an entire civil service of lesser deities. There were court officials such as the Transcendent Dignitary, a sort of celestial doorkeeper. There were masters of the elements, including a Count of the Winds and a Lord of Lightning. One particularly exalted figure was the Supreme Ruler of the Eastern Peak, supervising a ministry of seventy-five departments. Another

Heaven and took up residence among the stars in the Great Bear constellation.

From that time until the imperial examinations came to an end in the early twentieth century, he was their presiding deity. Candidates would keep his image, holding a writing brush and an official seal, in their home, and across China many millions of anxious prayers rose up to him in the tense days before the final assessment.

Kui Xing, the distraught scholar, is carried from the ocean to safety on the back of a strange sea creature.

105

powerful deity was the bird-headed Thunder God, who was responsible for punishing serious crimes through the emissaries of his Ministry of Thunder.

The Local Gods

If these gods filled the upper ranks of the celestial hierarchy, millions more operated on a purely local level. Among the most influential were the Cheng Huang, literally Gods of Wall and Moat, who were in charge of cities and rural districts. Like their Earthly equivalents in the imperial administration, they received petitions from local officials and were thought to report to the Jade Emperor on the daily activities of the areas under their control.

These celestial posts were often filled by deceased mortals, for the boundaries between the worlds of the living and the dead were always fluid. The Chinese had no problem imagining exemplary individuals continuing to provide posthumous service in the celestial sphere, rather like Christian saints in Heaven.

One example was Yue Fei, a real-life hero who in Song times led the imperial armies against invaders who had occupied northern China. Having won some notable victories, he sought to push on and reclaim the conquered lands, but was opposed by a peace faction eager to end the war. Gaining the upper hand, they had Yue Fei executed. After his death, however, he came to be revered as a hero of national resistance and was recompensed for his untimely end by being worshipped as the city god of Hangzhou, the capital to which the Song emperors had retreated.

Like Earthly magistrates, the Cheng Huang had many junior officials reporting to

Hell was a concept introduced to China by Buddhism, and Yama, the Hindu ruler of the dead, was the inspiration for Yan Luo, the prince of the Fifth Court of Hell, seen judging in a 14th-century painting. Those who stirred up enmity between relatives were sentenced to be gnawed by dogs.

The Kitchen God, Zao Jun, decorates this 1895 calendar. An image of this popular deity is traditionally put up over the stove every New Year, the old one being taken down the week before and burned using alcohol to make the god happy and try to ensure a favorable household report in Heaven.

them. Chief among these were Bai Lao-Ye and Hei Lao-Ye, Mr. White and Mr. Black, who kept watch by day and night respectively. Below them was a whole district administration of local deities with specific responsibility for each street, temple, bridge or village.

The process of supervision did not stop outdoors. Inside the house was the domain of the Five Genii, responsible respectively for the front and back entrances, the well, the inner courtyard and the aisles around which traditional Chinese homes were constructed. The front doors in fact had two tutelary deities, the Men Shen, one for each panel. Pictures of the guardians, typically dressed as fear-

some warriors, were pasted in place each New Year. Legend traced their origins to a Tang emperor who fell ill as a result of the attentions of a spirit; to drive it away, two army officers kept vigil at his door day and night, until he had the idea of having their pictures painted on the panels to let them get some sleep.

Most intrusive of the domestic spirits was Zao Jun, the Kitchen God. Each year he went to Heaven to make a detailed report on the behavior of the household over the previous twelve months. To avoid censure, each family member had to abide by a dizzying number of rules and regulations that stretched from avoiding blasphemy through showing proper respect for elders to maintaining high standards of hygiene. Bribery could also help: on the eve of the god's departure, he would be offered glutinous sweets and rice in the hope that his lips would stick shut.

For the pious, these reports were highly significant, for they were taken into account when each individual was judged after death. Beliefs about what happened in the afterlife varied considerably by region, and were further complicated by Buddhist notions of reincarnation. In general, however, it was thought that the soul of an individual who had behaved fittingly and whose memory was cherished with proper ritual observations would live on happily in the spirit world.

A very different fate attended those whose allotted lifespan was cut short unnaturally or who had no relatives to tend their graves. They risked turning into *gui*, restless ghosts condemned to wander the Earth for the balance of their given days. *Gui* of people who had committed suicide were especially feared, for they were believed to tempt others to follow their example so they could steal their bodies for reincarnation.

Thronged with gods, Immortals, ghosts and demons, the spirit world was above all crowded. And for believers it was ever-present. The numinous was never farther away than the nearest roadside temple or household shrine, and the divine hierarchy was quite as intrusive as the Earthly civil administration that it resembled.

Tales of the Eight Immortals

Daoists taught that those who achieved perfect union with life's essence could achieve immortality. The stories of eight, otherwise very ordinary, individuals who had attained that goal helped to popularize the message.

The secret of eternal life preoccupied the Chinese from the earliest times. Ancient myths spoke of two separate paradises in which the laws of aging did not apply. One lay in the fairy domain of the Queen Mother of the West, in whose garden grew a miraculous peach tree whose fruit brought immortality (see box, pages 78–79). The other was on islands in the Eastern Sea, the best-known of them vase-shaped Penglai. The First Emperor was sufficiently convinced of Penglai's existence to send an expedition in search of it in the year 219 BCE; none of the noble youths and girls who went on it were ever seen again.

The Daoist Disciplines

The Daoists made the quest for eternal life a central tenet of their faith. Over the centuries devotees set their minds to finding practical ways of achieving the necessary mystical union. They devised and systematized a range of techniques designed to lengthen life and, ultimately, to enable adepts to win immortality through spiritual perfection. The assumption underlying all such practices was the correlation of the microcosmic body to the macrocismic universe. One must identify and preserve the "primordial breath" (*yuanqi*) that corresponds to the life-giving, undifferentiated Dao at the beginning of creation. Retaining the vital bodily essences of "breath" (*qi*), "life-force" (*jing*) and "spirit" (*shen*), one could reverse the gradual depletion of these essences that otherwise led to death.

A wooden carving of Shou Lao, God of Longevity and a former star deity, holding a peach as the symbol of long life.

The reversal of aging was accomplished by various methods. In meditation and visual exercises, the practitioner focused on the Dao or on powerful astral gods residing in heaven and the body. Therapeutic and strengthening movements were also used to invoke these. Breathing techniques aimed to produce breathing that is so shallow and slow that a feather placed on one's nose would remain motionless. Select diet enhanced the purification of the mind and body: one consumed foods associated with long life, such as certain mushrooms, pine seeds and pine sap, and avoided foods that encouraged the "three worms" of disease, aging and death.

True Daoists condemned attempts to find a shortcut to a state properly achieved by spiritual discipline. Those who made these, they maintained, could expect short shrift from the law-enforcing emissaries of the Ministry of Thunder. It was probably in an attempt to popularize the Daoist message that stories of the Eight Immortals first started to circulate. Representing a cross-section of Chinese society, the octet brought home the message that victory over death was within anyone's grasp provided they had the motivation and will-power necessary to attain it.

No one knows for sure when the eight were first linked, though it seems to have been quite late in mythological terms, perhaps not before the fourteenth century. They soon caught the popular imagination, not least because they were portrayed in an approachably human way; several, for instance, had a partiality for wine. In time their images became ubiquitous, shown on every kind of decorated object from tableware to fans and wall-scrolls. They were generally depicted as a jolly group, contentedly enjoying for eternity the merited fruits of their labors.

Although the chronology of the group was always vague, the first to attain immortality seems to have been Li Tieguai, invariably depicted as a cripple with a crutch. After living an ascetic life for forty years, he was visited by the spirit of Laozi, the founder of Daoism, in human guise. Laozi tempted him with the pleasures of the flesh, and when the sage disdained them he was rewarded with immortality.

Some commentators claimed that Li had been born a cripple, but a more popular tale maintained that he acquired his crutch in the course of his initiation. In this version, Li told a disciple to look after his body while his spirit went to answer a summons from Laozi, instructing him to burn it if he did not return within the week, for he would in that case have finally become pure spirit. For six days the young man kept vigil, until word reached him that his own mother was dangerously ill. Not wishing to leave the body of his master unattended, he decided to proceed with the cremation a day early, assuming that his master had attained the immortality he sought.

But Li's spirit did return, only hours after the young man had left, and found only a pile of ashes where its human home had been. Looking around for an alternative to the body that had gone up in smoke, Li found an old beggar who had died on the mountainside a few hours before and he gratefully took up residence in the corpse, only to find to his chagrin that his host not only looked disreputable in the extreme but also had a lame leg. Seeing Li's discomfort, Laozi gave him in recompense a golden headband and the crutch that was to become his symbol.

Li held no grudge against his erring disciple. Proceeding at once to the young man's house, he found preparations already in train for the mother's funeral, but was nonetheless able to revive the corpse with his ever-present medicines. In later years pharmacists adopted him as their patron in recognition of his healing powers, and his image often adorned their shop signs.

If Li Tieguai represented China's sick and disabled, Zhongli Quan was a soldier and a man of action. After rising to be a Marshal of the Empire

An Unlikely Journey

Usually the Eight Immortals flew on clouds or cranes from their island home of Penglai. But on one occasion they decided to travel by sea, borne on a strange variety of different objects.

Each of the immortal eight used their own particular emblem to carry them over the waves.

Thus equipped, the cripple Li Tieguai straddled the crutch that had been given to him by Laozi, while the pot-bellied Zhongli Quan floated luxuriously on a feather fan with a horsehair tassel. Lü Dongbin, who is the best-known of all the Eight Immortals, surfed from Penglai on his magic sword, and Zhang Guolao trotted amphibiously on his paper mule, a magical beast that could travel thousands of kilometers in a day, yet when not required could be folded up and stored in a wallet like a piece of paper. The scholar Han Xiang, being associated with the ability to create blooms, paddled across in a flower-basket, while the only woman, He Xiangu, was wafted gently on a lotus leaf. Most improbably of all, the street musician Lan Caihe perched precariously on a pair of castanet-like clappers, while Cao Guojiu was borne very authoritatively on the official tablet that guaranteed the right of admission to the imperial court.

Chinese artists enjoyed exploiting the humorous aspects of this bizarre flotilla, which became a favorite subject for paintings and illustrations.

Storytellers subsequently adorned accounts of the trip with tales of hostile encounters with dragon-kings and sea monsters, and in time the expedition even provided a popular theme for opera.

These 19th-century southern Chinese tiles depict two of the Eight Immortals: He Xiangu (*left*) who lived off powdered mother-of-pearl and moonbeams, and Lan Caihe, theatrical patron, travelling on castanets (*right*).

in Han dynasty times, he retired to the mountains to pursue a hermit's life. As he was meditating in his cave one day, its stone walls split asunder to reveal a jade casket. Inside, Zhongli found documents of magic formulas that revealed the secrets of immortality. He followed the instructions they contained while the cavern around him filled with sweet sounds and multi-colored mist. Then a white crane arrived to carry him to his new home on the island of Penglai.

Lan Caihe was the most ambivalent of the octet, a wandering street musician sometimes depicted as a man and at others as a woman; in the theater, he was usually played by a male actor wearing female dress. On Earth he earned his living as a mendicant street musician, dressed in rags and wearing only one shoe. He acted like a madman, but the songs he sang showed him to be a holy fool, singing of the vanity of life and all its pleasures. Often he would throw away the money he was given, leaving it for those poorer than himself. He finally attained immortality in a fittingly bohemian way, passing out drunk in a tavern in Anhui only to be wafted off to the Island of Immortals, leaving behind his shoe, robe, belt and musical instruments.

The fourth Immortal, Zhang Guolao, seems to have been based on a real-life hermit of that name who lived in the seventh century CE. Word of his sanctity reached the Tang emperors, two of whom summoned him to appear at court, though on each occasion he refused to go. Eventually he was persuaded by the Empress Wu, only to fall dead at the gates of a temple as he entered the capital.

In the world of Daoist sages, however, death was not necessarily final. Although witnesses maintained that they had seen his body decay, he nonetheless turned up again not long afterward back in the mountains. He took to claiming that he was immemorially old, having served as a minister of the legendary Yao almost 3,000 years previously. Called to court once more by Emperor Xuan Zong, who acceded to the throne in 712 CE, this old man of the mountains performed various magical feats that included making himself invisible, drinking a

A woven silk rank badge from the early 16th century, worn on the coat to signify an official of the first rank. The bird depicted is a white crane, the animal that symbolized longevity and happiness. White cranes were normally used by the travelling Eight Immortals on their journey from Penglai.

cup of poisonous aconite and felling birds and flowers simply by pointing a finger at them.

In 735 Zhang was elected Chief of the Imperial Academy at Luoyang in Henan Province. At about that time, the emperor asked a celebrated Daoist, Fa-shan, to reveal the secret of Zhang's extraordinary longevity. Fa-shan protested that to do so would be more than his life was worth. When the emperor insisted, he agreed only when promised that Zhang himself would be brought to revive him. The Daoist then just had time to reveal mysteriously that Zhang's true form was that of a primordial white bat before apparently expiring, as he had predicted. Zhang subsequently agreed to restore Fa-shan to life – a feat he accomplished by sprinkling water on the face of the corpse. Shortly afterward Zhang returned to the mountains, where he himself finally died, though when his disciples opened up his tomb they supposedly found it empty.

In art Zhang is usually shown riding on a magical donkey. In later years he was venerated by married couples as a guarantor of fertility.

The only woman among the eight was He Xiangu. As a girl she was instructed by a spirit in a dream to powder and eat some mother-of-pearl. She did so, simultaneously taking a vow of chastity, and thereby gained the power to float in the sky at will. She spent her days in the mountains picking herbs and berries that she took home each evening to her mother, having herself lost the need to eat. Like Zhang she was summoned to court by Empress Wu, but she disappeared en route, having achieved immortality.

Lü Dongbin represented the administrative class among the Eight Immortals, and his legend reflects Daoist views of the vanity of pursuing a career. The story went that he came from a family of high officials; his father had been a government prefect. He went to the Tang capital of Chang'an to study, and graduated with honors. He was destined for high rank in the civil service when a chance encounter in an inn outside the city changed his life for ever.

There he encountered the Immortal Zhongli, dressed in human guise as a retired army officer. The two men struck up a conversation, ending up drinking together late into the evening. Eventually the alcohol and the heat of the inn made Lü drowsy. As his companion warmed another bowl of rice wine, he drifted off to sleep and had a remarkable dream.

In it, his future career seemed to unfold before his eyes. He saw himself rising from an obscure provincial posting to attain high office. He proved a wise and just administrator, and was rewarded with great honors. After many years' service he was looking forward to a contented retirement when one day someone complained to the emperor about some misdemeanor he had committed. To his horror, he saw himself disgraced and sent to live

Empress Wu Tian, first empress of China from 624 to 705 CE, was an imperial concubine until her marriage to Emperor Tang Gaozong. She summoned two of the Eight Immortals to court, Zhang Guolao and He Xiangu.

out his old age in lonely exile. Worse still, his entire family was summarily executed.

At this terrible moment Lü woke up in a panic to find that his companion was still heating the bowl. This "rice-wine dream," as it became known, was enough to convince the young man of the futility of the course he had previously set for himself. Instead he gave up everything to follow Zhongli. Having passed all the spiritual tests his master set for him, he was rewarded with a magic sword with which he travelled around China fighting the forces of evil and helping the oppressed.

One tale of his wanderings tells how he took the form of an oil-seller to seek out just individuals, intending to reward all customers who proved honest in their dealings. Sadly, everyone he came into contact with turned out to be either venal or grasping, until eventually he met an old woman who was content with the measure he gave her and did not try to cheat on the payment. In recompense, he cast a handful of rice into her well, which from that day ran with fine wine, making her wealthy.

The best-known of all the Immortals, Lü was credited with the authorship of many treatises and was even honored as the legendary founder of a Daoist sect. Artists often portrayed him with a male child in his arms and, ironically enough, couples came to venerate him in the hope that their children, unlike him, would turn out to be successful government officials.

Han Xiang, the seventh of the group, was also a scholar. He studied under Han Yu, a famous Tang dynasty statesman and poet who was reportedly his great-uncle, and soon came to excel his master; one story tells how Han Yu scoffed at Han Xiang's claim to be able to make flowers bloom instantaneously, only to be silenced when Han magically produced blossoms from a clod of earth. On the leaves, a verse appeared in golden letters predicting Han Yu's fall from favor – a prophecy that came true in real life, for the scholar ended his days in exile. Han Xiang subsequently attained immortality with the help of instruction from Lü Dongbin, receiving as his emblem a basket of the flowers he had miraculously created.

The last member of the group was Cao Guojiu, an aristocrat normally depicted in official robes, bearing a tablet indicating his prerogatives as a courtier. As a young man he was at best thoughtless, and allowed himself to become involved in the misdeeds of a wicked younger brother who ended up by implicating him in a sordid murder case. Lucky to escape execution, he renounced the life of a spoiled aristocrat to take refuge in the mountains, where he devoted himself to meditation. In so doing he attracted the attention of Zhongli Quan and Lü Dongbin, who revealed the secrets of eternal life to him and welcomed him into their fold as the eighth Immortal.

Complete at last, the group retired to the Island of Immortals in the Eastern Ocean. Over the centuries, poets and storytellers embroidered their legends, and devotees came to venerate them. In time they became the models of a long and happy life; the very number eight, by association, came to be a lucky one.

With their fondness for drink and helping deserving causes, the Eight Immortals were widely loved by the people and this was reflected by their prominence in popular art. Here, all of the Immortals are portrayed on a 19th-century tile wearing their distinctive garb and holding their respective emblems.

Patrons of the Professions

Every trade, craft and profession had its own guardian deity, and artisans would take care to pay them due respect if they wanted to prosper in their careers. As recently as the first half of the twentieth century, most Chinese guilds had a patron god; a survey in Beijing in 1924 found that only four out of twenty-four approached were without one.

Typically, an altar of the deity would be displayed prominently at all meetings, and members would kowtow before it on arrival. At the conclusion of business they would "send off the god" by burning handwritten prayers and offerings of paper money before it. Once a year they would stage a parade of colorful images of the god through the streets.

In some cases the gods were familiar mythological figures. Pharmacists, for instance, venerated Shen Nong, China's second emperor who was said to have discovered healing plants (see page 46). Tailors honored Huang Di, the Yellow Emperor, while potters offered their devotion to the deified founder of Daoism, Laozi.

Other patron deities had significance only within their own guild. Often they were humans reincarnated for their merits into the heavenly realm. So Luo Zu, sponsor of hairdressers and corn-cutters, was said to have been a disciple of Laozi's who gave up the religious life to become a street barber, while Ge Hong, patron of the dyers, was known in real life as the author of treatises on the alchemical transmutation of metals and on preparing the elixir of life. He was also the first person to give a written account of the Pan Gu creation myth (see pages 30–33); some scholars even believe he invented it.

One of the best-loved figures was Lu Ban, who was sacred to carpenters and builders. In the many folktales that gathered around his name he was usually depicted as a wandering artisan materializing unexpectedly to give counsel to builders faced with insurmountable problems. He was also credited with many useful inventions, among them the ball-and-socket joint and the trestled frame known as the carpenter's horse.

Purveyors of Wealth

Few deities are more assiduously courted than the Gods of Wealth, still honored each New Year with feasts, offerings and cheerful cries of "Rejoice and grow rich!"

Cai Shen is the best-known wealth god, and a legend of Ming times links him with Zhao Kongming, a hermit who lived at the time of the wars marking the downfall of the Shang dynasty. Abandoning his mountain retreat, Zhao enthusiastically backed the Shang cause, riding on a tiger's back and throwing pearls that exploded like bombs. The opposing Zhou general eventually had him killed by witchcraft, although he was later ashamed of the ignoble way in which he had dispatched the brave Zhao and proclaimed him in the name of the Daoist gods to be president of the celestial Ministry of Riches.

More likely candidates were two Immortals called He, popularly thought of as half-brothers, who started a business together but then fell out. For seven generations their heirs feuded before a benevolent deity brought the rivals together again, greatly increasing the prosperity of the family as a whole.

Legend claimed that he too had really existed, in his case in one of China's warring states in the third century BCE. When his father was executed for a crime that he had not committed, Lu Ban erected a statue of the dead man with his finger pointing toward the city where he had suffered injustice. Taking the message, the gods inflicted a terrible drought on it. In their misery the citizens begged for forgiveness, and Lu Ban, taking pity on their suffering, cut off the accusing hand. At once the curse was lifted and rain fell.

Another patron deity who remains popular to this day is Tian Hou, goddess of sailors. The stories claim that she was born into a fishing family along China's southern coast in the tenth century CE. As a girl she dreamed one night that the boat on which

Even today Tian Hou remains popular with the local fishing community (*above*) in her native southern China. In Hong Kong a festival is still held to this day in which her image is paraded through the streets to the sound of cymbals and firecrackers.

her father had gone out fishing was sinking in a high sea. Waking to find that a storm was indeed raging, she rushed out to the cliff's edge and pointed a finger imperiously at the sea. The next morning, when calm had returned, her father's ship returned safe but alone; all the others had been engulfed by the tempest.

In time Tian Hou came to be worshipped as a goddess, and over the centuries many stories told how she had appeared miraculously to save drowning men or to rescue vessels in distress.

115

The Outlaw God

In the fluid world of Chinese mythology, many human heroes were translated after death to the ranks of the gods. But none achieved such popularity as the war god Guan Di who rose to prominence as a "Robin Hood" figure, forced outside the law by injustice.

Guan Di's original name was Guan Yu. He was born in the last, lawless years of the Han dynasty. From the start, he was a wild youth, and his parents had difficulty controlling him. After one escapade they confined him to his room, but he soon found a way out. Wandering the streets, he heard a couple tearfully lamenting their fate. He stopped to find out what the matter was, and learned that their only daughter had been taken as a concubine by a local official, even though she was engaged to be married.

Outraged, Guan Yu promised vengeance. He went straight to the official's house and killed him. With his own life now at risk, he had to flee the city. He decided to head for the province of Shaanxi, warlord territory where he would be beyond the reach of the law.

After many adventures he found his way to a town near Beijing, where he had an encounter that changed his life. He noticed a local butcher – a giant of a man named Zhang Fei – storing his unsold stock down a well that he capped with a gigantic boulder, saying jokingly that any man who could shift it would deserve the meat. Taking him at his word, Guan Yu lifted the stone without difficulty and proceeded to help himself.

The butcher was furious, demanding his goods back. The two would have come to blows but for the intervention of a third man, an itinerant sandal-maker called Liu Bei who managed to restore the peace. The three started talking and soon found they had much in common, not least a hatred of rebel lords and a wish to see imperial control restored. There and then they decided to swear an oath of eternal friendship, dedicating themselves to the service of justice and

the emperor. Ever after they were known as the Brethren of the Peach Orchard, from the place where they took the pledge.

Thereafter the trio lived up to their word, taking on usurpers and warlords in a doomed attempt to save the Han empire. Raising a force of volunteers, they confronted the dreaded Yellow Turbans, rebels who had raised the flag against imperial rule.

In time the three went their separate ways, but they never forgot their obligations to one another. Once Guan Yu was taken prisoner, and his captor cunningly tried to compromise him by forcing him to spend the night in the same room as two of Liu Bei's wives, who had also been seized. To avoid any shadow of suspicion from attaching to them, Guan Yu spent the entire night standing in the doorway with a candle so that he could be seen at all times by those outside. Even his enemy was impressed by this display of probity, and came to respect Guan Yu as a man of integrity and honor.

Guan's Luck Runs Out

For all his efforts, Guan Yu was backing a hopeless cause, and gradually his luck ran out. By then he had a son to fight alongside him, but the two were encircled in the city of Maicheng by a fresh usurper, Sun Quan. With a handful of followers they made a last, desperate attempt to escape.

Under cover of darkness they rode through the city gates. They managed to break through the first line of attackers, but all along the road that led from the city Sun Quan had placed fresh detachments to capture them. They forced their way through half a dozen ambushes, but at last were taken alive. Sun Quan made a final attempt to persuade Guan Yu to change sides, but the hero dismissed his appeal contemptuously. So father and son were executed, side by side. Guan Yu's loyal steed refused to leave his master's body, standing guard over it until it too died.

Though Guan Yu was dead, he was not forgotten. Tales of his exploits passed down from generation to generation and in time he came to be regarded as the epitome of loyalty and honor.

As a defender of the imperial cause, he was as popular with China's rulers as with the people, and in 1120, 900 years after his death, he was awarded the rank of duke, upgraded eight years later to prince.

His posthumous career reached a climax in the sixteenth century, when his life provided the subject for an immensely popular novel, *The Romance of the Three Kingdoms*. Eventually, in 1594, the Ming emperor elevated him to the ranks of the gods as Guan Di, God of War. His cult spread rapidly, and soon there were temples to him in every major Chinese city.

Warfare in ancient China was a particularly brutal affair, involving massed bodies of men on foot hacking and hewing with halberds and other edged weaponry. Dagger-axes were favored weapons for this type of hand-to-hand combat. This bronze kui dagger-axe is from Eastern Zhou and dates from the Warring States period. It is decorated with a relief taotie monster-face decoration and a geometric pattern common to weapons from Sichuan and the north. Guan Yu's heroic exploits meant he was revered by people forever after, but as much for his ability to prevent conflict as for his martial prowess.

Lords of the Waters

Immortal and irascible, the aquatic dragon kings ruled China's seas, lakes and rivers, living at the bottom of the waters in the winter. Yet they could be friendly to those who paid them due respect, bringing the vital gift of rain during spring and summer.

One old tradition linked the kings with sexual potency, for the dragon was considered to be the epitome of the male principle, yang. They were also held to be the ancestors of the emperors of ancient times. A curious story told how a king of the legendary Xia dynasty once collected foam from the mouths of two of his forebears who appeared to him in dragon form. For many centuries the saliva was locked away in a box. When it was finally opened by the tenth ruler of the Zhou dynasty, it spread out magically through the palace. Recognizing its procreative potential, the emperor ordered all of his wives to undress in its presence, and several of them subsequently became pregnant, thus creating a direct link between the exist-ing ruling family and the monarchs of China's remote past.

Equally ancient was the notion that dragons could mount the clouds to bring rain. During droughts, peasants would take images of the dragon kings from the temples to show them the damage being done to their crops. In Han times, their images in clay would be taken out to the fields to encourage precipitation. They could also help harness rivers in time of floods; as late as 1869, an imperial edict giving thanks that an impending catastrophe had been averted reported that, "When the dikes of the Yellow River were in imminent danger of collapse, the repeated apparition of the Golden Dragon saved the situation."

The most powerful dragons were those who ruled the seas, rivers and lakes, and the mightiest of all were the sovereigns of the five oceans. Like the serpent-kings of Indian myth, they were thought to live in crystal palaces beneath the waves, feeding on opals and pearls. Once a year they travelled to Heaven to report to their celestial overlord, the Jade Emperor. Yet for all their powers, they were not invincible; Chinese myths were full of stories of heroes such as Nezha and Monkey (see pages 120–122 and 128–130) who stole a march on them but managed to avoid retribution.

Only exceptional individuals ever met the sea dragons face to face, but lesser mortals occasionally encountered their counterparts in the lakes and rivers. A story from the fifth century CE

A water dragon decorating the screen wall of the Palace of Peaceful Longevity in the Forbidden City. The king of all scaly creatures, the dragon is said to live underwater half the year, rising into the sky during the spring when the constellation of the Dragon is at its height.

The Foolish Dragon

Dragons were powerful beasts, but the legends also often portrayed them as stupid. One told how a sea creature on a mercy mission was easily outwitted by a monkey.

One day a dragon living in the ocean saw that his wife was unwell. Hoping to restore her health, he asked if there was any particular food that she would like to eat. At first she refused to answer, but when pressed confided that she had a craving for a monkey's heart.

The husband was at a loss to know how to satisfy her whim. Still, not wanting to see her suffer, he made his way to the shore, where he spied a monkey in the treetops. To tempt it down, he asked if it was not tired of its own forest, offering instead to carry it across the ocean to a land where fruit grew on every branch.

Easily persuaded, the simian climbed onto the dragon's back. It soon had an unpleasant

surprise, however, when the dragon dived down into the ocean depths. Panic-stricken, it asked where they were going, at which point the dragon explained apologetically that he needed a monkey's heart for his sick wife.

"Then you'll have to go back to land!" shouted the monkey desperately. "I left my heart in the treetops!"

Obediently, the foolish dragon did as he was told, swimming back to the shore and letting his prey scamper back to the trees. Scrambling rapidly to the safety of the topmost branches, the monkey thought to itself as it watched its former captor waiting in vain below: "What simpletons dragons must be to fall for a story like that!"

described how a girl gave shelter to a homeless old man one stormy night, only to find subsequently that she had become pregnant. She eventually gave birth to a formless lump of flesh which, when she threw it into a nearby lake, turned into a white dragon. The shock killed her, though her memory was kept alive in future years at the White Dragon Temple in Jiangsu Province.

A parallel tale told how, in Tang times, an individual named Liu Yi met a young woman mourning by the roadside. When he stopped to question her, she revealed that she was the youngest daughter of the dragon king of Dongting Lake, in northeastern Hunan Province. She was

unhappy because she had been repudiated by her husband, the son of a river god, and had had to take human form. Learning that Liu Yi was heading toward the lake, she gave him a letter for her father to inform him of her plight.

In his palace on the lakebed the monarch read the missive with deep concern. Instantly a dragon was dispatched to rescue the maiden, returning with her within moments. It turned out that the girl's husband had died in the interim so, in gratitude to Liu for bringing news of his daughter, the monarch offered her to him in marriage. The couple returned to the human world to live together as man and wife.

The Childhood Of Nezha

In the cycle of legends surrounding the supplanting of the Shang dynasty by the Zhou in the eleventh century BCE, no hero was more formidable on the battlefield than the supernaturally born Nezha. But the tales also revealed that the mighty warrior had been an extraordinarily difficult child.

Nezha's birth befitted a hero. His mother bore him for forty-two months without coming to term. Then one night she dreamed that a Daoist priest had entered her room. She indignantly demanded what he was doing, at which point he thrust a bundle into her hands and departed. She woke her husband, a military commander named Li Jing who at that time was fighting for the Shang cause. As she told him about the dream, she was seized by labor pains. The baby was on its way at last.

Her husband left the room to wait outside. He was soon interrupted by two maidservants who rushed out crying, "The baby's a monster!" Seeing a strange red light issuing from the bedchamber he charged in with drawn sword to find a ball of flesh rolling across the floor. He struck it with his blade and it split in two to reveal a beautiful baby inside.

The infant seemed healthy, but had come into the world with two unexpected accoutrements: a golden bracelet on his right wrist and a piece of red damask silk on his stomach that glowed with a golden light. These were magical gifts for, as the parents were soon to learn, the child was an avatar of a Daoist Immortal, Tai Zhenren.

The next day the sage descended from his mountaintop retreat to visit the proud parents. He told them to call the boy Nezha. "When he is older, I will take him as a disciple," he said.

Nezha was a precocious child, and by the time he was seven he was nearly two meters tall.

The Kunlun Mountains were the holiest range in Chinese mythology and it was here, with the Dragon King, that Nezha's father, Li Jing, studied the holy Daoist mysteries

Out one day with a servant, he stopped on a riverbank to moisten his silken cloth, intending to wipe his brow. But this was the Sky-Stirring Damask, and a single touch was enough to make the entire river boil and foam. The shockwaves spread outward to the Eastern Sea itself, rousing the concern of Ao Guang, the Dragon King, in his palace under the waves. He sent a guard to find the cause of the commotion. But Nezha took against his envoy and when the officer remonstrated with him, he threw the magic bracelet at him, killing him instantly.

Worse was to follow. When the officer failed to return, the king sent one of his own sons to investigate. Nezha dispatched the prince too, cutting out a tendon to turn into a dragonskin belt.

Ao Guang was enraged. Taking human form, he went at once to Li Jing's fortress to demand justice for his dead son. It turned out that the two knew each other, for both had studied the Daoist mysteries in the holy Kunlun Mountains.

At first Li Jing refused to believe that his child – a mere infant – could have committed so horrible a crime. But when Nezha was called for questioning, he made no attempt to deny the killing. Apologizing

with a bad grace to the Dragon King, he offered perfunctorily to return his dead son's sinew. The monarch strode out in a fury, telling Li Jing that he would take his complaint to the ruler of Heaven, the Jade Emperor himself.

Li Jing and his wife were inconsolable, and Nezha felt sorry for the grief he had caused them. Uncertain what to do to retrieve the situation, he decided to use his magical powers to visit his spiritual master Tai Zhenren at his mountain retreat.

The sage took the news of the killings philosophically, pointing out that they were predestined to happen. Drawing a magic symbol on Nezha's chest to make him invisible, he instructed him to go to the Jade Emperor's palace to waylay the Dragon King before he could make his complaint.

Nezha did as instructed. When he saw his accuser approaching the palace gates, his anger boiled over and he struck the Dragon King down, ripping away some of his scales in the process. As a final indignity, he threatened to kill the sea-monarch with his magic bracelet, just as he had his son, unless he agreed to drop his complaint.

Under duress, Ao Guang had to accept. But he had no intention of letting the matter drop. Confronting Li Jing with news of the latest outrage, he informed him that he now intended to make a joint complaint to the Jade Emperor in company with the Dragon Kings of the three other seas.

Meanwhile Nezha had been getting into further trouble. Finding a bow in the fort, he loosed off an arrow at random. But it was a magic bow, provided by a local deity for the protection of the defenders, and its arrows always struck home. This one flew all the way to the mountain retreat of the goddess Shi ji Niang-niang, killing a servant.

Now Nezha had two enemies among the ranks of the Immortals. He fled to Tai Zhenren but the goddess pursued him. When Tai refused to hand him over, the two celestial beings came to

121

Nezha made his second enemy among the gods when he loosed a magic arrow found in the fort and it killed a servant in the household of the goddess, Shi ji Niang-niang. These bronze arrows were found in the tomb of the First Emperor.

blows. Nezha's master finally prevailed by throwing over the goddess a magical coverlet of nine fire-dragons, which turned her to stone.

Yet Nezha's troubles were still far from over. Returning home, he found the four Dragon Kings on the point of carrying off his parents for punishment. To save them, he offered if necessary to pay for his misdeeds with his life. When they agreed, he duly disembowelled himself with a sword.

Released from its body, his spirit flew straight back to Tai Zhenren. Once more the Daoist master received Nezha kindly, but told him he could not stay; his cell was not fated to be the young hero's home. Instead he instructed him to appear to his mother in dreams, urging her to build a temple in which his soul could rest. By the rules of reincarnation he could expect to be given a new physical form after three years.

Nezha's mother did all that was expected of her, and soon her son's shrine became a popular place of pilgrimage, famed for the miracles that were performed there. Eventually word of it reached Li Jing, who had still not forgiven his son for his crimes. When he learned that the patron spirit of the place was none other than the errant Nezha, his anger knew no bounds. Rushing to the sanctuary, he smashed up the sacred images and told the worshippers gathered there to find a more worthy object for their devotions.

Nezha's spirit was absent at the time of the attack, and when he returned he was appalled to learn what had happened. Flying instantly to Tai Zhenren, he demanded his help. Knowing that Nezha's services would be required in the forthcoming struggle to overthrow the Shang dynasty, the Immortal agreed once more to aid him.

First Tai had to complete the unfinished process of reincarnation that Li Jing had interrupted. He did so with the aid of two water lilies and three leaves. Forming a human image with the plants, he proceeded to breathe life into it, and up rose a youth of gigantic stature, five meters high. Then the sage provided the young warrior with weapons: a lance tipped with fire, two Wind-Fire Wheels that could carry him anywhere in an instant, and a golden brick in a panther-skin bag.

The first person on whom Nezha chose to try out his armory was his father Li Jing. But Tai Zhenren intervened to tell the pair that they had greater foes to confront and a more important task to accomplish. Forcing Nezha to promise to live in harmony with his father in future, he gave Li Jing a magic weapon too: a golden pagoda that could envelop any enemy in flames. Then he announced that father and son must prepare themselves by meditation and austerities for the coming battle. For Li Jing was to command the heavenly hosts against the tyrant of Shang, and Nezha would be his principal assistant.

The Demon-Eater

A legend of the Tang dynasty told how one tormented soul repaid a debt of gratitude to the imperial family by protecting its members from other, more malicious spirits.

The Tang emperor Ming Huang had a fever, and one night a demon assailed him in his troubled sleep. The imp was fantastically dressed in red trousers and a single shoe. Having broken into the palace through a bamboo gate, he was irreverently gambolling through the state chambers playing a flute, showing none of the respect due in those sacred precincts.

Angrily, the emperor asked him what he thought he was doing. "My name," he replied, "is Emptiness and Desolation." The ruler was looking around in vain for a guard to remove him when suddenly a fearsome apparition rushed in, wearing a tattered robe and a torn bandanna. The newcomer seized the demon, crushed it into a ball and swallowed it.

Startled, the emperor enquired whom he had to thank for his deliverance. The spirit replied that his name was Zhong Kui, that he had lived in Shaanxi Province in the preceding century, and that he had been unjustly deprived of first-class honors in the public examinations. In his anger he had committed suicide on the steps of the imperial palace; but instead of treating his corpse with ignominy, as his behavior had merited, the reigning emperor had ordered it to be buried ceremoniously in a green robe – an honor normally reserved for members of the imperial family. Out of gratitude, Zhong had vowed to protect his successors for all time against the demons of despair.

At that point the emperor woke up to find that the fever had left him. He subsequently described the apparition to a court artist, who painted a portrait of Zhong Kui that was still hanging in the imperial palace 300 years later.

The Goddess of Mercy

The best-loved of all China's Buddhist deities was Guan Yin, the Goddess of Mercy, an abbreviation of a longer Chinese name that means "listening to the cries of the world." In her Earthly incarnation, this model of compassion was a devout and long-suffering princess named Miao Shan.

The title was, in fact, a mistranslation of the name of a male Indian bodhisattva named Avalokitesvara ("Merciful Lord"). In China he came to be thought of as a female (Miao Shan), illustrating the way in which the Daoist and Buddhist pantheons became amalgamated in the popular imagination.

Miao Shan's father, Miao Zhuang, was a usurper who had seized control of a kingdom by force of arms. Having won power, his one wish was for a male heir. But the gods were angry with him for his brutal ways and refused to answer his prayers. Instead they gave him and his wife three daughters, of whom Miao Shan was the youngest.

Miao Zhuang was distraught, but his chief minister tried to cheer him by pointing out that he could choose husbands for the girls, thereby selecting his own heirs. The king took some consolation from that thought, and in due time he found suitable partners for the two eldest. But when it came to Miao Shan's turn, she refused to marry, telling her father that she

A figure of Guan Yin, made in 1564. Scholars believe that several different divinities contributed to the cult of the goddess, first introduced to the Chinese pantheon as a deity inspired by Avalokitesvara.

wished only to renounce the world and enter a Buddhist nunnery. Her father was outraged by her defiance, but the more he insisted the more she vowed she could take no joy in an existence dominated by the Three Woes of old age, sickness and death. In the face of her stubbornness the king eventually pretended to give way, permitting her to enter a nunnery of his choosing. But he instructed its superior to make her life a misery, thinking that the hardships inflicted on her would soon make her lose her vocation.

Through fear of the king the abbess consented, and Miao Shan was given every unpleasant, menial task the place had to offer. But the gods looked down on her suffering with compassion, and the Jade Emperor himself gave instructions that she should receive divine assistance to carry out her duties.

When the superior reported to Miao Zhuang that the gods themselves were helping his daughter, he flew into a rage. Unused to being thwarted in any way, he determined on a dastardly deed: he ordered his men to burn down the nunnery. But the gods intervened again, sending a rainstorm to douse the flames and save the lives of the inmates.

For Miao Zhuang this was the final straw. Realizing his daughter would never bow to his will, he gave orders for her execution, reckoning that nothing but death provided suitable punishment for her disobedience.

Once more, however, the gods came to her aid. When the executioner tried to behead the girl, his sword shattered. A lance thrust at her broke into pieces. Eventually she was strangled with a silken cord, but the moment that her soul left her body a huge tiger appeared from nowhere and carried off the corpse to a nearby pine forest. The beast was actually a local god in disguise, sent by the Jade Emperor to keep the body unharmed and moisten its lips with the Elixir of Life in order to protect it from decay.

Shortly afterward Miao Shan's spirit, which had left the body at the moment of death, woke up in unfamiliar surroundings. The princess found herself in a desolate and featureless wasteland that a

shining spirit-being soon told her was Hell. However, it added, she had nothing to fear; the gods of the infernal regions had heard of her sanctity, and simply wanted to see proof of it with their own eyes.

In fact they got more than they bargained for, for Miao Shan's prayers soon turned Hell itself into a veritable paradise. Alarmed, the gods sent messengers to their Supreme Ruler to complain that the divinely instituted order was being overturned. He hastily commanded that her spirit should be taken back to her Earthly body, which was still lying uncorrupted in the pine forest where the tiger had left it. From there, reborn, she was transported magically to Xiang Shan, a holy island far to the south where many Immortals lived.

Miao Shan spent nine years in this sacred place, practicing meditation and self-discipline until she attained perfection as a bodhisattva or future Buddha. The gods themselves came to celebrate her achievement.

Meanwhile, the evil done to her by her father had not been forgotten. To punish him, the Jade Emperor afflicted him with painful ulcers. The sores gave him no rest, tormenting him night and day. He sent courtiers throughout his kingdom and beyond in search of a cure.

Word of his malady reached Miao Shan, and she decided to go to his aid in spite of all the wrong he had done her. Assuming the disguise of a wandering priest-physician, she went to his palace incognito and asked to see the king, assuring the guards that she knew a way of curing him.

The ruler was sceptical at first, and his incredulity turned to anger when she told him the vital ingredient in the ointment that would heal him: the hands and eyes of a willing volunteer. But before he could have her thrown out of the palace, she assured him that such a person existed, on the island of Xiang Shan. At once the king dispatched his minister Zhao Zhen to find out if what the priest said was true.

Zhao Zhen left at once, leaving two people at court who were less than happy to hear of his mission. Miao Zhuang's two sons-in-law had no desire

The Vanishing Monastery

A Buddhist tale told how a wandering contemplative spent a night in a ghostly retreat. The monk, named Ban Gong, got lost while he was travelling through the hills on the way to a monastery.

Evening was falling, so he was delighted to hear a bell ringing through the shade. Following the sound, he came to a complex of buildings proclaimed by a sign above the entrance to be the Monastery of Spiritual Retirement. As he approached, guard dogs barked at him, but a monk beckoned him in.

Inside, the whole place seemed deserted. The central hall was laid out as a dormitory, but there were no personal belongings to be seen. Most of the doors going off the hall were locked, but eventually Ban Gong found one that opened onto a small cell containing a bed. It too appeared to be unoccupied, so he decided to stay there for the night.

Some time afterward, he was disturbed by voices from the main hall. Looking out, he was astonished to find that it was filling up with monks entering not through the door but from the ceiling, floating down like feathers from a hole in the roof. From their conversation it became apparent that they had flown to the site from many parts of China and from India, too.

Hearing someone mentioning a famous Zen master's name, Ban Gong interrupted the gathering to say that he had studied under the man. At the sound of his voice, the whole spectral host disappeared along with the buildings, and the monk found himself alone once more on the hillside. Continuing on his way, he came at last to a real monastery. There he learned that reports of the vanishing cloister had been made for centuries, though few ever knew more of its presence than the tolling of an unseen bell.

to see the king cured, for they had been waiting for him to die to take over the throne. Now they determined on desperate measures. They plotted to kill the monarch in his chief minister's absence, along with the priest who threatened to cure him.

Accordingly, they prepared a poisonous drink for the king and sent it to him with an assurance that it came from the priest. But Miao Shan, with the omniscience of sainthood, learned of their evil intent and used her magic arts to transform the poison into a harmless broth.

Shortly afterward, when the assassin the princes had hired entered the priest's room with murder in mind, Miao Shan's spirit left the victim's body to travel back to Xiang Shan. As the murderer struck the now-lifeless form with his dagger, the priest's robe rose of its own accord from the bed, entangling him inextricably in its snares. He was found in the room the next morning by palace guards, and under torture soon revealed full details of the conspiracy of which he had been a part. The two sons-in-law were instantly executed; as for the would-be assassin, he was cut into 1,000 pieces.

Meanwhile Zhao Zhen had reached Xiang Shan, where the priest's instructions led him to Miao Shan. He was astonished to see the princess, whom he had long thought dead, but was even more amazed to learn that she herself was the

A late 18th-century figurine of the merciful Miao Shan under whose influence Buddhist lohans became increasingly identified with Daoist Immortals. It was said of this mother goddess that her milk filled the ears of the rice plant.

volunteer who was to surrender her eyes and hands. He did his best to dissuade her from this gruesome act of self-sacrifice, but she ordered him not to obstruct the will of Heaven. At her bidding, he himself cut off her hands and gouged out her eyes. Sightlessly, Miao Shan transformed the gory remains into an ointment that the minister bore as quickly as possible back to the king.

The balm instantly restored the monarch's health, and when he learned the identity of his benefactor his gratitude and wonder knew no bounds. Won over at last by the power of his daughter's compassion, he announced that he would go to her at once to thank her.

When he reached Xiang Shan and saw her mutilated form, he flung himself to the ground and announced that he was giving up the throne, nominating the faithful Zhao Zhen as his successor. Then, turning to Miao Shan, he said that his only remaining wish was to stay on the island as her disciple, if in the fullness of her mercy she would have him.

As an Immortal, Miao Shan could control her bodily form, and she chose that moment to appear miraculously whole again before them. She gladly welcomed her repentant father into the true path. And the Jade Emperor himself, who had been looking down benignly on all that happened, sent word that, for her devotion and compassion, she herself should henceforward be worshipped as a Buddha.

127

The Monkey King

Starting out as a Buddhist satire on the Daoist pantheon, the tale of the monkey who ended up as a god received the ultimate accolade when its hero himself became the stuff of legend.

The story of the Monkey King has no parallel in world mythology. To begin with, it is the work of a known author, even if little is recorded about him other than his name, Wu Cheng'en, and the fact that he was writing in the sixteenth century. Then again his book, *The Journey to the West*, has an odd pedigree, borrowing its title and its basic premise from a factual work of the same name written centuries before.

This first *Journey to the West* described the actual pilgrimage made by the monk Xuanzang to India in the seventh century CE to bring the Buddhist scriptures back to China. Wu Cheng'en's reworking was very different – a wildly comic fantasia spanning the entire mythological cosmos, including Heaven and Hell, in which the monk acquired some very unlikely travelling companions. By a final irony, the most resourceful of these – a monkey with vast supernatural powers and a human body – became so popular throughout China that he himself became an object of veneration; images of him even cropped up in temples.

The plot of the book – best known in the West through an English version, *Monkey*, prepared by the poet and translator Arthur Waley – is so thickly packed with incident that no summary can do more than sketch its outlines. It starts with the birth of Monkey – no ordinary simian, for he emerged from a stone egg high up on the Mountain of Flowers and Fruit. The Jade Emperor himself gave

A Ming-dynasty jade monkey. The Journey to the West is an allegory in which Monkey represents human failings.

him special powers that soon caused him to be declared King of the Monkeys. But after ruling his kingdom for many years, Monkey decided to go in search of wisdom. He met up with a Daoist Immortal, who took him on as a disciple and taught him how to fly through the air and to transform himself into seventy-two different shapes. He also learned how to cover 50,000 kilometers in a single leap, and to create 100,000 duplicates of himself simply by pulling out some hairs and crying, "Change!"

Armed with his new powers, he returned to the monkey kingdom and organized his subjects into an army 47,000 strong. But he still wanted a weapon for himself, and to find one he went to the court of the Dragon King under the Eastern Sea. There he tricked the monarch into giving him a magic wand that could change its size at its owner's behest. It could swell into a mighty pillar stretching to Heaven or shrink to the size of a needle that Monkey could conveniently store behind his ear.

The Dragon King complained of the theft to the Lord of Hell, who sent minions to arrest Monkey while he was drunk at a feast. When he came to, he was less than happy to find himself in the infernal regions and threatened to use his wand to destroy them unless he was set free at once. He made such a nuisance of himself that his captors were glad to let him go, even though he insisted on removing the pages of the *Register of*

the *Living and the Dead* containing the entries for himself and all his monkey subjects before he left.

Monkey was making powerful enemies by his raucous behavior. Now the Lord of Hell joined the Dragon King in presenting a formal complaint to the Jade Emperor. Pusillanimously the Ruler of Heaven decided that the best way to keep his obstreperous subject out of further trouble would be to give him a menial post in the heavenly kingdom itself. So Monkey was summoned to the royal presence and granted the fine-sounding title of Grand Master of the Heavenly Stables.

He accepted the post with gratitude, but it did not take him long to realize that his only task was to feed the emperor's horses. Outraged at the

The Four Kings of Hell correspond to Buddhism's Four Diamond Kings of Heaven who guarded the Register of the Living and the Dead that Monkey stole when he was carried off to Hell.

offense to his dignity, he stormed off back to Earth, where he proudly proclaimed himself to be the Great Sage, Equal of Heaven. To punish his presumption, the Jade Emperor sent an army to arrest him, but this was repulsed. Monkey then threatened to invade Heaven unless his new title was recognized. Alarmed, the emperor sought to buy him off with a grander position. This time he was appointed Grand Superintendent of the Heavenly Peach Garden.

129

The Queen Mother of the West astride a sacred phoenix and holding one of her peaches, in a detail from a *kesi*. Appointed to watch over the peaches, Monkey went and ate all the best ones.

This posting, too, turned out to be a disaster. First Monkey ate all the best peaches of immortality the Queen Mother of the West had been growing for the Peach Banquet she gave once every 3,000 years. Then he gatecrashed the festivities themselves before any of the other guests arrived, eating and drinking all the finest delicacies. Finally, tipsy and bloated, he found his way to the palace of Laozi, the deified founder of the Daoist religion, where he swallowed the golden pills that contained the Elixir of Life.

Now doubly immortal, Monkey escaped back to Earth with all the hosts of Heaven pursuing him. He led them a merry dance, but eventually he was taken. Yu Di's rage knew no limits, and he gave orders that the miscreant should be executed immediately. But that proved impossible; the pills and peaches had made him invulnerable as well as immortal, and warriors hacked at him with axes, poked with lances and smote him with swords to no effect.

Eventually Laozi himself offered to get rid of him in his alchemical furnace. But that too proved ineffective; even after forty-nine days, the crucible did no more than make Monkey's eyes smart.

In despair, Yu Di handed his charge over to the Buddha, and here at last Monkey more than met his match. When he boasted that he was powerful enough to rule Heaven itself, the Buddha challenged him to prove it by a simple test; all Monkey had to do was jump out of the Buddha's hand.

The task seemed easy enough. Monkey used all his powers to soar upward for nearly 60,000 kilometers. Eventually he came to five huge pillars reaching up into the sky. Assuming that they marked the farthest limits of the universe, he left evidence of his presence by urinating on the base of one of them. Then he returned in triumph. But the Buddha only laughed to see him back. The five pillars had been the god's own fingers, and the smell emanating from one of them was proof enough that Monkey had never left his grasp.

Thereafter, Monkey was imprisoned for his misdeeds for thousands of years, trapped under a mountain range. He was released through the intercession of Guan Yin, Goddess of Mercy, only on condition that he fulfil his destiny by accompanying the Buddhist monk Xuanzang to India to bring the Buddhist scriptures back to China. To restrain his natural violence, the goddess put a band on his head that tightened on command, instantly giving him a splitting headache.

The story of the journey quickly turned into a serio-comic epic. Along the way the monk and Monkey acquired two unusual travelling companions. The first, Pigsy, had been banished to Earth from Heaven for violating a daughter of Yu Di, and had been reincarnated as a monster with a man's body and a pig's face. The second, another fallen celestial official, had taken the name of Brother Sand and supported himself by waylaying and murdering travellers until offered the chance to redeem himself by joining their quest.

This unlikely quartet endured no fewer than eighty separate adventures between them on the journey to the West, surviving them all through the combination of Xuanzang's holiness, Monkey's sharp intelligence and the brute strength of Pigsy and Brother Sand. Eventually, after fourteen years, they reached their destination and collected the scriptures from the Tathagata Buddha himself. In completing the pilgrimage, Xuanzang acquired the power of flight, which considerably shortened their return journey; they were able to make their way back to the Chinese court in just eight days.

There they delivered the holy books to the emperor, and Heaven and Earth joined to proclaim the success of their mission. As Xuanzang read from the scriptures, the four, plus Xuanzang's white stallion, slowly levitated into the air, while the courtiers fell to their knees in wonder.

They ascended into the presence of the Buddha, who pronounced the fates awaiting them.

Pigsy was appointed Head Altar-Cleaner to the gods – a post that, as the Buddha reminded him, would give him plenty of opportunities to finish off the scraps of ritual offerings. Brother Sand, who had shown real signs of reformation, became a saint in Heaven. As for Xuanzang and Monkey, they received the greatest accolade of all, winning the status of Buddhas.

Monkey was left with only one concern: to be rid of the migraine-inducing band that Guan Yin had put around his head. When Xuanzang asked him gently if it had troubled him recently, he raised his hand to his temples. Only then did he realize that it had disappeared of its own accord along with the last traces of his animal nature.

A Close Shave

Journeying in search of the Buddhist scriptures, Monkey and his companions faced many dangers. One requiring special ingenuity was the Land that Hated Priests.

On learning that the inhabitants of the land they were entering killed all priests who crossed their borders, the four Buddhists first tried to disguise themselves by donning native clothing. To assure their safety further, they spent the night locked inside a wardrobe in a roadside inn. But robbers came and stole the cupboard, only to abandon it soon after when challenged by policemen.

The travellers' plight now seemed desperate; their true identity was sure to be revealed by their priestly tonsures when they were found the next day. But Monkey, thinking fast, found a solution. Using his magical powers, he created 1,000 monkeys just like himself and provided each one with a razor. Between them they shaved the heads of all the land's leading citizens while they slept. In a land of bald-headed men, the pilgrims' own bare scalps subsequently went unnoticed.

THE POWER OF QI

Energy or life-force was known to the Chinese as qi and existed in both animate and inanimate objects. Humans had to live in harmony with their environment in order to have the correct amount of qi in the body; imbalance caused disease. Similarly, feng shui was the art of arranging things in accordance with the forces of the universe; buildings had to be located in propitious places and designed so as to harness the qi in the natural world. Qi itself was divided into the oppositional forces of yin and yang, which were in turn composed of the Five Elements that made up all living things (see page 19). Certain forms of physical and mental exercise were practiced to balance the elements in the body and regulate the flow of qi to benefical effect; indeed, Qigong and Tai Ji, or T'ai Chi, are still used today. The art of feng shui meant getting qi to stay but not stagnate and to flow but not dissipate.

Above: While Tai Ji exercises were used to improve bodily qi, the manifestation of illness was attributed to evil spirits dissipating it. Coin swords such as this one were used to ward them off.

Left: An undated chart details particular acupoints or places to exert pressure on, or needles into, the kidney meridians – the name given to the network of channels in the body along which qi flows. There were a dozen major meridians, in six yin and yang pairs, each reflected by a different bodily pulse (six on each wrist). Most meridians related to the five organs that govern bodily qi; illness resulted from a blocked or unruly flow of qi.

Left: Feng shui took its name from the words for "wind" and "water," the firm and soft, yang and yin aspects respectively. The theories it was based on were outlined in the Yi Jing and developed into the geomantic art for which this compass, or Luo Pan, was used. Aligned to magnetic south, planetary and calendrical data were read and a site's qi level assessed.

Below: These images of people in various Tai Ji ("supreme ultimate") poses are from a silk book called *Daoying Xing Qi Fa* that dates from c.168 BCE. The exercises formed one of the Five Excellences. Tai Ji's focus was internal, concerning the mind and relaxation. The solo exercises were based on the movements of different animals.

THE CHINESE LEGACY

All mythologies reflect the societies that produced them, but few have ever been as closely enmeshed with the governing system as that of dynastic China. The nation's legendary heroes were emperors or servants of emperors, and even the Daoist Heaven itself borrowed its endlessly proliferating hierarchies of gods from the imperial court and administration.

So when the Chinese Revolution of 1911–12 brought an end to imperial rule, the reverberations were immense. Suddenly stories depicting the sovereign as a semi-divine being conspiring with ancestors who were themselves gods for the people's welfare lost their relevance. Even Confucian tales praising filial piety and deference to authority seemed suspect, for Confucianism had been the official ideology of the old ruling class. In the wake of the last emperor's abdication, some traditionalists made a half-hearted attempt to establish it on a fresh basis as a mass religious movement, but the effort petered out for lack of support.

In the new intellectual climate, the educated classes had little time for the traditional tales. The new ideologues were obsessed with China's backwardness, which had led to national humiliation at the hands of technologically more advanced powers. Their watchwords were "Science" and "Progress"; for them, the old stories smacked of the China they wanted to leave behind.

So when, after the chaos of the warlord era that followed the overthrow of the Manchus, the Nationalist Party of Chiang Kai-shek began to assert its authority, it made campaigning against "superstition" one of its priorities. It adopted a "Procedure for the Abolition of Divination, Astrology, Palmistry, Geomancy and Magic," and ordered sellers of incense, candles and other merchandise to find new jobs. Although the Nationalists were happy enough to allow Daoist temples dedicated to sages and past worthies to operate unhindered, orders were given that those devoted to legendary gods should be suppressed. In practice, however, the policy was never widely enforced. A few urban shrines were converted into schools, but in the countryside the old beliefs survived little changed, or in some cases even strengthened by the need for havens of hope in time of civil war.

When Mao Ze Dong's Communists came to power in 1949, attitudes to the myths hardened. Yet Mao himself said that superstition could not be suppressed by force, and religious freedom was written into the constitution of the People's Republic, although religious organization was strictly controlled.

When the Communists came to power in 1949, the constitution granted religious freedom. But the regime was nonetheless avowedly atheistic, and all references to gods or immortals were stripped from the school curriculum. At the same time, temple lands were handed over to the peasantry, leaving priests who had formerly lived off endowments to find a new source of income.

Anti-religious sentiment in China rose to a peak in the turbulent days of the Cultural Revolution. In the late 1960s, priests and temples became prime targets of the campaign against the Four Olds: old culture, old ideas, old customs, old habits. Most shrines simply closed their doors for the duration, not to reopen until after Mao's death in 1976. At the same time, the war on superstition also intensified. Communist Party officials sponsored rallies in the countryside at which geomancers and Daoist healers were challenged to produce the spirits with which they claimed to communicate; when these failed to materialize, they were forced to confess publicly that they had been making a living through deception.

Yet despite its anti-religious bias, Maoism was far from hostile to all aspects of China's mythological heritage. As a ruling ideology, it inherited a strong didactic streak from earlier times, and Maoist ideologues, like their Confucian predecessors, soon came to see legends and folktales as excellent channels for transmitting salutary messages to the masses. Mao himself had a particular enthusiasm for stories about peasant outlaws, equating their exploits with his own struggles in the days when the Communist Party was proscribed. As a ruler he also found something in common with legendary monarchs such as the Sage Kings who had devoted their lives to rescuing the Chinese people from floods or famine.

As a result, folklore studies received something of a fillip. In the first flush of enthusiasm following the 1911–12 Revolution, scholars had fanned out through the countryside collecting the songs and stories of the people, but these activities had gradually fallen out of favor under the Nationalists, who considered such material primi-

The Shengmu Temple in Taiwan, where places of worship and mythic beliefs have remained undiluted by Communism.

tive and backward. Under Mao, folktales were once again cherished as the people's literature, and their simplicity and directness were contrasted favorably with what now came to be seen as the stilted elitism of imperial Confucian culture.

Only some aspects of the tales were acceptable, however, and editors and anthologists had to take care to ensure that the message they conveyed was politically correct. The introduction to one popular anthology of the Communist era spelled out what was considered admirable. Admissible tales praised labor, as when Nü Wa created humankind or the divine archer Yi travelled around China righting wrongs. They extolled the tireless spirit of heroes, like Yu the Great who spent years taming floods devastating the nation without once returning home. They glorified the struggle against tyrants, notably in the tales of the downfall of the Xia and Shang dynasties. And they expressed the longing of the common people for love, marriage and family life in legends like the Cowherd and the Girl Weaver (see pages 64–65).

135

Myths that did not fit these categories were simply passed over. In the words of one Western expert, "Stories containing much mythological material and stories praising the emperor, the imperial bureaucracy, or male heroes" were largely left out, in favor of others extolling the common people or women.

Folktales and legends also served to pass on appropriate messages. One of the world's oddest anthologies of ghost stories was the 1961 publication *Stories of Not Being Afraid of Ghosts*, which aimed to combat superstition by featuring only tales in which evil spirits were routed by resourceful peasants. In the field of legend, the first part of the Monkey King saga (see pages 128–131), in which the hero takes on the celestial powers-that-be, was diffused as an example of resourceful rebellion; but the latter section, in which he travels to India to bring back Buddhist scriptures, was regarded as less edifying and was often omitted.

Also, traditional retellings were adapted to accord with current attitudes. When the hero of *The Romance of the Milky Way*, a perennially popular dramatic version of the Cowherd and the Girl Weaver story, told his bride-to-be, "We must pick

Chinese Vengeance was produced by the Shaw Brothers in 1972 and was set during the Qing dynasty. It was one of a genre of films that incorporated themes of individuals confronting tyranny and used Buddhist-inspired martial arts characters.

an auspicious day to be married," she was now made to correct him gently with, "You are still a little superstitious. No day is as good as today."

Yet the very fact that such dramas were still performed was proof that the myths were still in demand. Throughout the Maoist period, comic books recounting the old tales in black-and-white line drawings continued to appear, even though they were occasionally confiscated by zealous Communist officials. Above all, the stories passed down by word of mouth from parents and grandparents to children, just as they had always done. And within the home there was little attempt to adapt them in the light of current political fashions.

Mythical Rebirth

The myths also survived undiluted among the millions of Chinese living outside China's borders. Taiwan, Hong Kong and Macao in particular provided enclaves where Daoist worship continued during the Cultural Revolution, when religion was all but forbidden on the mainland.

In addition, Hong Kong helped to introduce the myths to new audiences through its flourishing film industry. The Shaw brothers and other producers raided old legends for the plot of films such as *The Mad Monk* and *Madame White Snake*, while ghost stories drawn from folktales also provided themes. In particular, King Hu's *A Touch of Zen* helped to popularize the figure of the Buddhist or Daoist monk with magical powers.

Since Mao's death, times have changed in mainland China, too. Though statistics are hard to come by, traditional religion has by all accounts staged something of a comeback; temples that had been shut down have reopened, the veneration of ancestors is once more in evidence and some traditional festivals such as New Year, when houses are cleaned and offerings are made to the Kitchen God, and Qing Ming, when graves are renovated, have been revived. Fresh accounts of the classic myths have been published, and the tale of Guan Di, once worshipped as a war god, has even been a popular television series. Reportedly there are even some new legends describing the miraculous

preservation of statues or shrines during the iconoclastic days of the Cultural Revolution.

At the same time, aspects of the culture that produced the myths have taken root further afield. The New Year festivities have found fresh homes in the West, and are colorfully celebrated wherever there are sizeable Chinese communities, from Los Angeles to London and Seattle to Sydney. Meanwhile, ancient esoteric practices have found a new audience among non-Chinese New Age enthusiasts worldwide. Ever since the 1960s, the *Yi Jing* – a 3,000-year-old book of divination that ranked among the Five Classics of the Confucian canon (see page 16) – has had cult status in the West among people in search of arcane and often ambiguous guidance on what the future might hold. And one of the least expected crazes of the 1990s has made feng shui, the ancient art of geomancy, a hot property in interior decoration and design circles internationally.

After surviving difficult times in the twentieth century, Chinese myths and the culture they reflect are in renewed health as a fresh millennium dawns. And if China itself continues to open up to the outside world, the chances are that they might soon find a whole new audience around the globe.

This apartment complex in Repulse Bay, Hong Kong, has been built next to a mountain, a place of yang where a dragon is believed to reside. The hole in the structure permits the dragon an unrestricted view of the sea, which earns its goodwill, and enables the beneficial qi of the mountain to enter the building.

Glossary

Ba gua The mystical eight trigrams and the key to knowledge, invented by Fu Xi.

bi Symbol for the circular sky or Heaven; *bi* discs often have a central hole for the *lie kou*.

bodhisattva A future Buddha, or one who has vowed to become a Buddha. Gautama Buddha himself was one until he attained Enlightenment.

dao Literally the "Way," a philosophical movement begun by Laozi and outlined in his work *Dao De Jing* (*Way and its Power*). Two of its core beliefs were a preference for nature and solitude over human society and an emphasis on *rang*. Eventually it embraced mysticism, magic and a return to nature.

feng huang The phoenix, which represented drought, the element fire, the cardinal direction of south and the season summer, and was identified with yin and the empress. Often referred to as the Red Phoenix or Red Bird of the South.

feng shui A geomantic art, the principles of which dictated that objects had to be arranged in accordance with the forces of the universe so as to harness the *qi* in the natural world: getting it to stay but not stagnate and to flow but not dissipate.

gui Restless ghosts condemned to wander the Earth for the rest of their days.

kesi Technique of weaving silk tapestries.

kui A dagger-axe used in combat.

li A measurement of distance that equates to just over 500 meters.

lie kou Chinese cosmogony identified this as the hole in the top of the sky through which lightning flashed.

lohan A carved representation, often in ivory, of one of the disciples of the Buddha.

qi Energy or life-force that existed in both animate and inanimate objects. It had to be harnessed correctly and an imbalance avoided.

qilin Strange unicorn-like animal hybrid and living embodiment of the union of yin and yang. An appearance by such a beast was usually an omen.

rang Part of Daoist belief, meaning yieldingness or a desire to "go with the flow."

taotie A form of relief decoration used on metal objects, particularly weapons, usually in the form of geometric, monster-face patterns.

wu A word with a variety of meanings, including the number "five," but in the context presented here it refers to "shaman, wizard or witch" and the magic and ritual practiced by China's old religious tradition.

wu-wei A "non-action" philosophy developed by Laozi and Zhuangzi that meant "action without contrivance."

xiao Obligations owed to parents by their children, reflected in the cultural importance of filial piety.

yin Female, absorbing quality associated with passivity and darkness. One of two opposing but complementary forces, the other is yang, that permeate all life and the universe and whose interaction is the very process of life.

yang Male, penetrating quality associated with activity and brightness. One of two opposing but complementary forces, the other is yin, that permeate all life and the universe and whose interaction is the very process of life.

zhang A measurement that equates to three meters.

zhu A bird shaped like an owl but with human hands that shows itself only in badly governed lands.

For More Information

The British Museum
Ancient China
38 Russell Square
England, WC1B 3QQ
Web site: http://www.ancientchina.co.uk
One of the most respected museums in the world, the British Museum's Ancient China exhibit features Chinese history, artifacts, and writings.

China Institute
125 East 65th Street
New York, NY 10065
(212) 744-8181
Web site: http://www.chinainstitute.org
Founded in 1926, the China Institute educates visitors about the art, history, and culture of China.

Chinese American Museum
425 North Los Angeles Street
Los Angeles, CA 90012
(213) 485-8567
Web site: http://www.camla.org
The museum is located in the last surviving building of the original Chinatown of Los Angeles. It is dedicated to research, education programs and exhibits about Chinese Americans in the United States.

Chinese Culture Center of San Francisco
750 Kearny Street, Third Floor
San Francisco, CA 94108-1809
(415) 986-2825
Web site: http://c-c-c.org
The center preserves and promotes Chinese art and culture for the American public through its exhibitions and educational programs.

The Crow Collection of Asian Art
2010 Flora Street
Dallas, TX 75201
(214) 979-6430
Web site: http://www.crowcollection.com
This collection is dedicated to the arts and cultures of China, Japan, India, and Southeast Asia.

Freer Gallery of Art and Arthur M. Sackler Gallery
Smithsonian Institution
P.O. Box 37012 MRC 707
Washington, DC 20013-7012
(202) 633-4880
Web site: http://www.asia.si.edu
The Smithsonian Institution's two museums of Asian art are the Freer Gallery of Art and the Arthur M. Sackler Gallery, which are connected by an underground passageway. Both museums are renowned for their innovative exhibitions and research facilities.

Seattle Asian Art Museum
1400 East Prospect Street
Volunteer Park
Seattle, WA 98112-3303
(206) 654-3100
Web site: http://www.seattleartmuseum.org
The Seattle Asian Art Museum is part of the Seattle Art Museum organization. It has a world-famous Asian collection of artwork, artifacts, and sculpture.

Web Sites

Due to the changing nature of Internet links, Rosen Publishing has developed an online list of Web sites related to the subject of this book. This site is updated regularly. Please use this link to access this list:

http://www.rosenlinks.com/wmyth/chin

For Further Reading

Birch, Cyril. *Chinese Myths and Fantasies*, Oxford University Press: London, 1961.
Blunden, Caroline, and Elvin, Mark. *Cultural Atlas of China*, Phaidon Press: Oxford, 1983.
Chamberlain, Jonathan. *Chinese Gods: An Introduction to Chinese Folk Religion*, Blacksmith Books: Hong Kong, 2009.
Chen, Lianshan. *Chinese Myths and Legends*, Cambridge University Press: Cambridge, 2011.
Christie, Anthony. *Chinese Mythology*, Paul Hamlyn: London, 1968.
Ebrey, Patricia Buckley. *Cambridge Illustrated History of China*, Cambridge University Press: Cambridge, 2010.
Gernet, Jacques. (trans. J.R. Foster) *A History of Chinese Civilization*, Cambridge University Press: Cambridge, 1985.
Granet, M. *The Religion of the Chinese People*, Blackwood: Oxford, 1975.
Hook, Brian (ed.). *The Cambridge Encyclopedia of China*, Cambridge University Press: Cambridge, 1982.
Jianing Chen, and Yang Yang. *The World of Chinese Myths*, Beijing Language and Culture University Press: Beijing, 1995.
Shaughnessy, Edward. *Exploring the Life, Myth and Art of Ancient China*, Rosen Publishing Group, New York, 2009.
Waley, Arthur. *Monkey* (abridged trans. of *Journey to the West*), Penguin: London.
Walls, John and Walls, Yvonne (ed. and trans.). *Classical Chinese Myths*, Joint Publishing House: Hong Kong, 1984.
Werner, ETC. *Myths and Legends of China*, Harrap: London 1922.
Yu-lan, Fung. (trans. D. Bodde) *A Short History of Chinese Philosophy*, Macmillan: New York, 1948.
Watson, William. *China*, Thames and Hudson: London, 1961.
Yang, Lihui and An, Deming. *Handbook of Chinese Mythology*, Oxford University Press: New York, 2008.

Index

Page numbers in *italic* denote captions. Where there is a textual reference to the topic on the same page as a caption, italics have not been used.

Photo Credits:

The publisher would like to thank the following people, museums and photographic libraries for permission to reproduce their material. Every care has been taken to trace copyright holders. However, if we have omitted anyone we apologize and will, if informed, make corrections in any future edition.

Key:

t = top; **c** = center; **b** = bottom; **l** = left; **r** = right

Abbreviations:

Bridgeman Art Library, London/New York = BAL
British Museum, London = BM
Christie's Images, London = Christie's
Duncan Baird Publishers = DBP
ET Archive, London = ET

Images Colour Library, London = Images
John Bigelow Taylor, New York = JBT
Robert Harding Picture Library = RHPL
Victoria & Albert Museum, London = V&A
Werner Forman Archive, London = WFA

Cover BAL/Oriental Museum, Durham University; **Cover surround** Christie's; **title page** ET/Bibliothèque Nationale, Paris; **contents page** Christie's; **page 6** Tony Stone Images, London/Christopher Arnesen; **7** Christie's; **8** RHPL/G. Corrigan; **10** Michael Holford, London; **11** Michael Holford, London/Museum für Volkerkunde, Munich; **12** DBP; **13** Christie's; **14** RHPL; **15** JBT; **16–17** BAL/Bibliothèque Nationale, Paris; **18** BAL/Oriental Museum, Durham University; **19** Images; **20** BAL/Bibliothèque Nationale, Paris; **21** BAL/Zhang Shui Cheng; **22t** BAL/Private Collection; **22b** BM/Seligman Bequest; **23l** Christie's; **23r** Christie's; **25** V&A; **26l** ET/Bibliothèque Nationale, Paris; **26r** Christie's; **27tl** Images; **27c** Seattle Art Museum/Eugene Fuller Memorial Collection/Paul Macapia; **27b** BAL/Freer Gallery, Smithsonian Institution, Washington; **28** Kaikodo Gallery, New York; **29** Christie's; **30** BM; **31** Michael Holford, London/Wellcome Collection, London; **32** RHPL/G.&P. Corrigan; **33** BAL/Freud Museum, London; **34–35** Christie's; **35** JBT; **36** Ancient Art & Architecture, London/Ron Sheridan; **37** Christie's; **38** BM; **40** Christie's; **41** Christie's; **42** BM; **44–45** RHPL/Robert Francis; **46** BAL/Fitzwilliam Museum, University of Cambridge; **48bl** V&A; **48r** Christie's; **49** National Maritime Museum, London; **50** BM; **51** Christie's; **52** Christie's; **53** ET; **54** JBT; **55** RHPL/DFE Russell; **56–57** BM; **58** Science & Society Picture Library, London; **59** Christie's; **60** JBT; **62** Christie's; **63** ET/V&A; **66** ET/Freer Gallery, Smithsonian Institution, Washington; **67** Christie's; **68** V&A; **70** Images; **71** ET; **73** Images; **74** V&A/Ian Thomas; **75** BAL/BM; **76** RHPL/Explorer, Paris; **77** JBT; **78–79** Christie's; **80** BM; **82** ET/National Palace Museum, Taiwan; **83** BM; **85** Magnum Photos, London/Bruno Barbey; **86** Christie's; **88** National Palace Museum, Taiwan; **89** ET/BM; **90–91** V&A; **92** ET/Musée Guimet, Paris; **93** Christie's; **94–95** RHPL/Dominic Harcourt-Webster; **98–99b** RHPL/Schuster; **99r** ET; **100t** ET; **100b** RHPL/G.&P. Corrigan; **101t** Magnum Photos, London/Inge Morath; **101b** BAL/V&A; **102** Asian Art Museum, San Francisco/Avery Brundage Collection (B62 D28); **103** Christie's; **106** Michael Holford, London/Horniman Museum, London; **107** BAL/Oriental Museum, Durham University; **108** Michael Holford, London/Wellcome Museum, London; **110l** Images; **110r** Images; **111** V&A/Ian Thomas; **112** ET/BL; **113** Images; **115** RHPL/Paul van Riel; **116–117** JBT; **118** Magnum Photos, London/Bruno Barbey; **120** RHPL/Nigel Gomm; **121** BM; **122** National Geographic Images Collection, Washington/O. Louis Mazzatenta; **124** Christie's; **127** Christie's; **128** Christie's; **129** Michael Holford, London/BM; **130** Asian Art Museum, San Francisco/Avery Brundage Collection (B62 D28 – detail); **132bl** Wellcome Institute Library, London; **132c** BM; **133t** Images; **133b** DBP; **134** BAL; **135** RHPL/Tony Waltham; **136** Ronald Grant Archive, London; **137** RHPL/Amanda Hall